POLAND AFTER SOLIDARITY

MINISTRY OF DEFENCE
H.Q. LIBRARY SERVICES

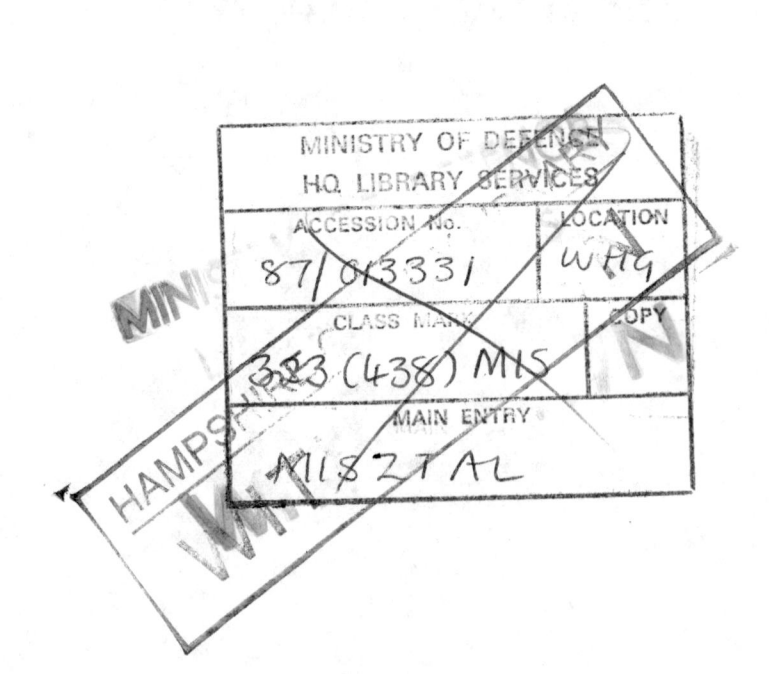

ACCESSION No.	LOCATION
87/01333/	WHG
CLASS MARK	COPY
323 (438) MIS	
MAIN ENTRY	
MISZTAL	

POLAND AFTER SOLIDARITY

Social Movements versus the State

Edited by

Bronislaw Misztal

Transaction Books
New Brunswick (U.S.A.) and Oxford (U.K.)

Copyright © 1985 by Transaction, Inc.
New Brunswick, New Jersery 08903.

All rights reserved under International and Pan-American Copyright Conventions. No part of this book may be reproduced or transmitted in any form or by any means, electronic or mechanical, including photocopying, recording, or any information storage and retrieval system, without prior permission in writing from the publisher. All inquiries should be addressed to Transaction Books, Rutgers—The State University, New Brunswick, New Jersey 08903.

Library of Congress Catalog Number: 85-2777
ISBN: 0-88738-049-2 (cloth)
Printed in the United States of America

Library of Congress Cataloging in Publication Data

Main entry under title:

Poland after solidarity.

    1. Poland—Politics and government—1980—
2. Social movements—Poland. 3. NSZZ "Solidarność" (Labor organization) I. Misztal, Bronislaw, 1946-
DK4442.P59   1985   322'.09438   85-2777
ISBN 0-88783-049-2

Contents

Preface..vii
Acknowledgments..ix
Abbreviations...xi

PART ONE SOCIAL MOVEMENT VERSUS THE STATE

1. Apathy-Participation-Apathy: The Vicious Circle of
   Collective Behavior in Contemporary Poland............................3
   Bronislaw Misztal

2. Solidarity and the State: Strategies of Social Reconstruction..........19
   Jack Bielasiak

3. Institutionalization of the Party-State Regime in Poland..............39
   Paul G. Lewis

4. Constitution and Functioning of a Civil Society in Poland............57
   Maria Markus

5. The Catholic Church in Defense of Civil Society in Poland...........67
   Bogdan Szajkowski

PART TWO BEYOND SOLIDARITY

6. Eastern Europe in the "Crisis of Transition": The Polish
   and Hungarian Cases..87
   Robert Manchin and *Ivan Szelenyi*

7. The State and the Legitimacy Crisis.....................................103
   Barbara A. Misztal

8. Resource Mobilization and Solidarity: Comparing
   Social Movements across Regimes.......................................113
   Elisabeth Crighton

9. Beyond Solidarity: Democratic-Symbolic Ruminations..............133
   Scott Warren

10. Social Movements against the State: Theoretical
    Legacy of the Welfare State...143
    Bronislaw Misztal

About the Contributors..165

Preface

Bronislaw Misztal

The unexpected emergence of the Solidarity movement in Poland has focused Western attention on conflicts within the socialist state. The rapid truncation of Solidarity and the rise of a new image of the state as a strong, relatively autonomous, repressive apparatus has left several theoretical questions unresolved. While recent publications address the issues that contributed to the rise and fall of an independent trade union in Poland, the structure of the state-movement relationship remains unexplained. This volume draws from historical and political accounts of the events that haunted Poland between 1980 and 1984, but it goes beyond description, attempting to provide a more complex sociological explanation of the major processes that occur within the state-society sphere of relationships.

From this perspective, Poland is seen as an extreme case of conflict between the state and society. Solidarity emerged in Poland as a powerful social movement to mediate that conflict. The movement failed and the responsibility for this failure must rest with specific political personalities. Societal dynamics, however, make progress in even the most inflexible regimes inevitable. That is why the movement's failure is not the end but the beginning of a long process of state development and accommodation to forces of societal change that will eventually delineate the new forms of state-society relations.

A number of qualitatively new structural processes occurred in Poland, not only between August 1980 and December 1981, but throughout the whole decade of the 1970s and after martial law as well. These structural processes require careful theoretical examination in order to provide an answer to the meaning of the Polish "revolution of hopes." The significance of the conflict between the movement and the state for other socialist countries and for the capitalist system must be explicated. While the military repression of Solidarity in Poland is inexcusable, there is little doubt that had a similar movement occurred anywhere else in the world, it too would have been truncated. Solidarity was born ahead of its time and, although the movement itself was doomed, there is a whole sphere "beyond Solidarity." The idea of the liberation of labor has a vital meaning for the future organization of productive and distributive activities that are traditionally organized by the state. The idea will undoubtedly recur periodically. The state's own apparatus, however, will always protect its monopolistic position. Social movements that emerge elsewhere in the world also challenge the monopoly of the state. This conflict is less dramatic only because of the pluralism of the means of articulation. The conflict between the social movement and the state may become even more bitter in the final decades of the twentieth century, which is why this book looks "beyond Solidarity" toward the twenty-first century.

This volume consists of two parts. In the first part, the conflict between social movements and the state in Poland is examined. The analysis of Solidarity's natural history provides a more orderly look at the stages of developments in the Poland of the 1980s. The nature of the political conflict between Solidarity and the Communist state in Poland is presented as a class conflict between society and the power elite. An analysis of the institutionalization of the means of control by the Party over society is provided. A systematic theoretical analysis of the functioning of civil society follows. The mediating role of the Catholic Church, which not only defends civil society in Poland, but also enriches the conflict, is likewise addressed.

The second part of the volume focuses on the issues that go "beyond Solidarity." A comparative analysis of three different upheavals (Hungary, 1956; Czechoslovakia, 1968; Poland, 1980) focuses on the scope of state autonomy and on how much may be gained by society. An analysis of legitimacy conflicts within socialist and capitalist states is provided. Other social movements which were overshadowed by Solidarity are analyzed in a comparative way. The philosophical symbolism of Solidarity is also examined. Finally, a theoretical interpretation of state interventionism discusses the structure of conflict induced by contemporary social movements.

Acknowledgments

By a happy coincidence I was invited to spend the 1983-1984 academic year at Pitzer College in Claremont, California. The college officials and the colleagues who voted to bring me to Claremont hoped to enrich the curriculum with a set of courses focusing on modern sociological theories of social movements, the state, socialist systems, and urban struggles. The intellectual tradition of Pitzer College, combined with a sort of academic laissez-faire among the students and faculty, promoted an increased interest in contemporary political issues. The question I was asked most frequently concerned the impact of developments in my native Poland on social and political movements elsewhere in the world. The speed with which Solidarity grew and then withered on the political landscape of Eastern Europe left several questions about its role and fate unanswered. More significantly, however, Solidarity's conspicuous popularity and the political vacuum it left behind stimulated questions about the lasting effects social movements may have on the political system, even when the movement is effectively truncated.

Confronted with so much intellectual interest, I decided to bring one or two speakers to the campus to address the most pertinent issues. College officials and colleagues were so positive about the project that imperceptibly it grew into a full-blown, two-session panel entitled "Social Movement versus the State: Beyond Solidarity." The panel included Andrew Arato, Jack Bielasiak, Adam Bromke, Andrew Janos, Andrzej Korbonski, Ivan Szelenyi, and myself as speakers, and Elisabeth Crighton, Fred Warner Neal, and Scott Warren as discussants. The panel revealed a need for further intensive theoretical work and I decided to compile a volume that would deal with conflictual relationships between contemporary social movements and states in general and the conflict between Solidarity and the Polish state in particular. For various reasons some of the original participants on the panel were unable to contribute to this endeavor. Fortunately, Paul Lewis, Maria Markus, Robert Manchin, Barbara Misztal, and Bogdan Szajkowski, with whom I had worked earlier, were willing to write additional chapters.

Acknowledgments

My thanks go to all who participated in the original panel and who contributed to this volume. It was an intellectual adventure for me to work with such a distinguished group of scholars. I am especially indebted to the people of the Pitzer College community. Ronald Macaulay, Dean of Faculty and Vice-President for Academic Affairs, was the first to be infected by my ideas for a conference and a book. His friendly assistance, measured by the allocation of funds both to bring the speakers and prepare the manuscript, made this whole endeavor possible, while his optimism, sense of humor, and diplomacy helped us to sail through several unexpected difficulties. The paternal protection of Frank Ellsworth, President of Pitzer College, who presided over the hottest debates of the conference, enabled us to retain some control over the divergent views of both participants and audiences. Glen Goodwin, chair of the sociology field group at Pitzer, used all his enthusiasm to disseminate the idea of the conference in the academic community of Claremont and throughout the West. Sue Keith, Director of Public Information, and Sarah Neiman, Associate Director of Development, spent infinite time and energy to provide the conference with a proper setting and adequate publicity. Stella Vlastos patiently typed major parts of the manuscript. A grant from the Pitzer College Research and Development Committee made possible my own contributions to this volume. I would also gratefully like to acknowledge the Fulbright-Hays academic award from the Council of International Exchange of Scholars and the U.S. Information Agency, which brought me to the United States.

Abbreviations

DiP — Experience and Future. A group of over 100 people, mostly intellectuals, whose collective views on the Polish crisis were published under the form of four reports.

CPSU — Communist Party of the Soviet Union.

KOR (KSS KOR) — Committee for Workers' Defense. Formed in 1976 by a group of intellectuals to defend the workers, who were persecuted after the strikes of 1976 in the cities of Ursus and Radom.

MKS — Interfactory Strike Committee. A body coordinating the strike in Gdansk in August 1980.

NSZZ — Independent, Self-Governing Trade Union, organized in August 1980, later known as Solidarity.

PAX — Association of Catholics. A progovernment organization of lay Catholics.

PUWP — Polish United Workers' Party. The ruling Communist party in Poland.

ROPCIO — Movement for Defense of Civil Rights.

SKS — Students' Self-Defense Committee.

WRON — Military Council of National Salvation. A military group formed in December 1981, known for its collective responsibility for the imposition of martial law.

Part One
SOCIAL MOVEMENT VERSUS THE STATE

1
Apathy-Participation-Apathy: The Vicious Circle of Collective Behavior in Contemporary Poland

Bronislaw Misztal

Poland has always attracted the attention of historians, politicians, and journalists because of the unpredictability of its history and its people. It has been labeled "God's Playground," for it is a country "where fate has frequently played mischievous tricks" (Davies 1982, xvi). From this perspective Polish society has often been seen as overwhelmed by its geopolitical location and by the fact that it is dominated by reasons of state characteristic of various European nations. Poles are believed to "have often behaved irrationally, taken the wrong options, or hurt themselves by a sometimes fatal inability to agree" (Steven 1982, xix). The dramatic history of the nineteenth- and twentieth-century uprisings raises serious questions about the consistency of specifically Polish collective behavior, governed by the structural inability of the society to bring about change without sequences of increased, inexplicable patriotic participation. In the Polish case patriotic commotion is usually followed by a period of apathy, when the immobilized society restructures itself in preparation for yet another uprising.

The unpredictability of the apathy-participation-apathy sequence does not stem solely from historical and geographic factors. It is also related to the internal structure of the institutions that govern Polish social and political life. The Roman Catholic Church, specifically Polish Catholicism, is deeply "embedded in the national fabric .... It has always exerted a considerable impact on popular attitudes towards political ideologies and institutions" (Szajkowski 1983, 1). While the church has traditionally been an important institution, the state, on the other hand, has traditionally suffered from weak legitimacy. One cannot analyze the sequences of collective behavior in Poland without consideration of this structural imbalance. In addition to its own internal logic, the collective behavior of Poles is subject to the influence of two institutions, the state and the church.

The purpose of this chapter is to unravel the stages of development of the social movement during the turbulent period of 1980-1984, using the natural history approach (Hopper 1950). The political stage in Poland was designed for more than one actor. Solidarity was just one element, although a principal one, in a complex play of interests, ideas, and political programs, and in a contradictory set of relationships among all the actors involved in this revolution of hope.

The Uniqueness of the Polish Revolution of Hope

The developments, that marked the coming of the 1980s in Poland attracted international attention, as if something entirely new had happened in socialist society. Despite a long tradition of worker unrest, both in Poland and elsewhere in the world, and the evidently widespread popular discontent with Communist leadership in Poland (Keefe et al. 1973, 167; Davies 1982, 2:625-33), many were surprised by the unprecedented emergence of Solidarity. What was remarkable was not the character of Solidarity as a social movement, but the fact that the movement emerged in a Communist-administered state. Such a state is supposedly governed by the principles of rational planning and overwhelmingly centralist control over the processes of social development (Misztal and Misztal 1984, 315-28). Unknown, unpredictable, and uncontrollable reality poses a threat to such a system. Pluralism in political life strengthens the unpredictability of social developments; therefore, diversity must be curbed, controlled, and leveled out to form very simple patterns of representation. Changes, if any, must be initiated by the center of authority and power. They have to come from above if they are not to raise political suspicion. A nation must become an "advanced socialist society" that comes to terms with Communist authority (Bauman 1971). The pace of political activity in such a society is usually quite slow, unless rapid and dramatic developments occur. But periods of upheaval are short and political "sobering" is usually implemented with the help of external might (Karpinski 1982).

The low level of participation and the apathetic mood of society are to be directed by the authorities. Only occasionally, during national elections, is even marginal activity tolerated or expected, but it must be extinguished as soon as the election is over.

Everybody was surprised, then, by the fact that an advanced socialist society ignored the external system of checks and balances imposed by the Communist power. The new civil society also ignored the alleged threat of intervention, as well as Cassandran predictions of new partitions of Poland. In fact, it ignored the totalitarian political system and exploded into a massive social movement. Although the Solidarity movement attracted the attention of both Poles and external observers, what really excited interest was the fact that the movement emerged in such an unusual environment, under such adverse conditions, and in such an unpredictable way.

In contrast with earlier Polish uprisings, the revolution of hope that took place in 1980 constituted a collective effort to bring about a totally new order. However insubstantial and unrealistic the preliminary program of Solidarity may seem from today's perspective, it differed from preceding uprisings in at least two ways. First, the new movement supported one general point of view that was based on a negation of the previous policies of the state. Second, the movement became an organized collectivity with a particular long-term goal, that is, the implementation of a qualitatively new, society-sponsored system of social justice and program of social development.

The following analysis will examine the crucial mechanisms involved in forming a social movement from what had originally been a sequence of collective behavior. Many of these processes and mechanisms are already identified in general theories of revolution and sociological theories of social movements (Blumer 1957; Davies 1962; McLaughlin 1969), but, as pointed out, the case of the revolution of hope that emerged in Poland in 1980-1981 was in many respects different from what might have been hypothesized. The second part of this paper examines some major social myths adopted by Solidarity itself as well as by the Communist powers. Some of these myths were widely accepted and contributed to the course of the natural history of the movement.

The Natural History of a Social Movement*

Social movements in many respects resemble human life: they are born and they die. The day they are born we wonder at the reason for their rapid emergence. The day they die, especially when effectively truncated, we seek the reasons for their rapid fall.

---

*At various points in this paper I shall draw on my earlier article: "Apathy and Participation: Natural History of Polish Solidary Movement." (Communist Affairs 3(1984).

Both questions mark the problems associated with the mobilized activity that lay behind the Solidarity movement. Ultimately, they also reflect the problem of the sudden indifference of the masses, who, when confronted by terror, pressure, and threats to survival, withdrew from overt action, restricting themselves to an intense display of moral support for their union.

Poland already has a long record of apathy and participation, exhibiting a paradoxical cycle: upheaval-apathy-upheaval. As noted by Starski (1982, 5-12), "the making of a new type of state in Poland met with relatively tame responses from most sectors of Polish society." The reason for this was the "debilitation" of two social layers, the peasantry and the workers, as a result of the mass destruction of World War II. Even before the genocide of the war, Polish society knew long periods of apathy, since it had lived under various partitions for more than one hundred years. The apathetic mood of Poles was broken by short periods of political activism and struggles for freedom (Karpinski 1982).

The rise and fall of Solidarity delineates two perspectives on Polish society. One is optimistic. It emphasizes the birth of Solidarity and stresses rising activism and participation by the masses. This perspective explains the genesis and early stages of the movement, while neglecting its potential truncation and fall. The other is pessimistic. It foresees a dramatic end, anticipating the doubt and despair of the more advanced stages of the movement's existence. This perspective explains the immediate reasons for the failure of resistance, while neglecting the immense desire of humans to live with dignity.

The actual developments oscillated between the extremes of unlimited growth of participation on the one hand, and the future, inescapable end of the movement, on the other (Starski 1982, 245-53). One could in fact describe the natural history of Solidarity as a sequence of several scenarios.

THE PRELIMINARY STAGE: SOCIETY AS A MASS
(June 1976-June 1980)

Dissatisfaction: The Discovery of Suffering
and Oppression

This stage began with the summer riots of June 1976. It was marked by major processes that may be labeled the dusk of humanism. Earlier attempts at upheaval, in March 1968 (in the case of students and intellectuals) and December 1970 (in the case of the working class), had reinvigorated individual political activity that had long been dormant (Karpinski 1982). The set of policies enforced by the new leadership in 1971 aimed at neutralizing major dissident grievances

(Keefe et at. 1973, 145-63). Since one of those grievances was the low purchasing power of workers, the new leadership of the Communist Party sought to identify itself with new values such as increased consumption. The idea was to attract individual attention to the possibility of enriching oneself through the systematic acquisition of material goods. Several economic decisions were made to convince the population of the reality of this new era. National industry started to produce new goods under technological licenses from abroad, and Party-run propaganda promoted visions of the wide availability of such goods. The symbols of this new era have become the Fiat automobile and color television. Although these and other goods were produced in large quantities, they were not universally available; access to them was controlled by the authorities through coupons issued only as a reward for some display of political conformity. Therefore, although the idea of consumerism was universally accepted by the population, it was effectively available only to a selected few. Subsequently, the society was divided into those who were able to acquire material goods, those who were on a waiting list, and those who had no chance of acquiring goods. The idea of consumerism effectively diverted the original spirit of the movement, directing it into materialist channels. The population was seduced by the pursuit of consumer goods and the increase of conspicuous leisure for the middle classes, which combined to demoralize all levels of social behavior. A general belief that anything could be bought and that what mattered was the price lowered moral standards and led to the development of greed and bribery as accepted means of adaptation to life in the "advanced socialist society." The morale of the nation declined and apathy appeared as a defense mechanism against demoralization. Several other mechanisms accompanied this process.

The development of class antagonism was unprecedented in postwar Poland. The conspicuous concentration of privilege within the class of professional apparatchiks became a new feature of the power elite. Originally, during the Gomulka period, apparatchiks were supposed to have power but neither wealth nor prestige. Gierek's era brought the tendency to use one's power as a means of exchange or extortion. Power was a means of access to scarce goods and, since consumerism was the driving force, those in power were able to acquire wealth or prestige in exchange for this access. The pursuit of academic careers by several Party officials is a good illustration of this search for both power and prestige. Unlike many other revolutionary situations, Poland experienced a concentration of both economic and political power. This process had important implications for future developments, since it created a clearly defined power elite willing to defend its concentrated privileges. The differentiation between "haves" and "have nots" was abundantly apparent in Polish society during the second half of the 1970s.

The chances for upward social mobility and channels for participation were blocked for those outside the establishment. Several preferential systems excluded working-class youth from the best high schools and universities. Similar preferential systems kept the average citizen off lists of housing recipients, as well as lists of executive jobs. Even after death people were still unequal, since privileges regarding funeral arrangements varied. The existing mechanisms of interest articulation, such as worker's self-management conferences, were already tightly controlled by the political apparatus, which orchestrated these activities to comply with the image of a unified nation.

Simultaneously it became apparent that although the government was effective in curbing spontaneity of social development, it was unable to implement any significant reforms in the economic and social systems. Endless meetings of the Central Committee of the Communist Party, wordy resolutions, and programs of economic maneuvering did not accord with the reality of life. The so-called administrative reform of 1973 was the only one effectively implemented by the authorities. Unfortunately, this reform destroyed the existing system for the execution of administrative decisions. In the second half of the decade it became obvious that the power elite was torn by factionalism, and the tentative credit given to Gierek's government was withdrawn. Moral restlessness, socialization to crisis, and an increased popular consciousness of the need for structural reforms prevailed in the society.

This period belonged to the dissident leaders who served as agitators, raising morale and sensitizing the masses to their social destiny. This period was also characterized by nominal organization of the masses' behavior, little interaction between social classes, and the lack of articulated ideology.

The papal visit in June 1979 marked a breakthrough and catalyzed new social processes that changed the course of events in Poland. It not only brought new hope and increased religious belief and morale, but also raised in the minds of the people the possibility of organizing society independently of the state. Papal authority and charisma brought about a new philosophy of life. The pope criticized the ideology of "labor for labor," pointing to the fact that increased efficiency would not lead to the freeing of individuals. He sowed the seeds of doubt in society; reflection followed. Reflection transformed the doubt into criticism.

The papal visit also marked another important development. For the first time since the Communists seized power in 1944, Poles were allowed to organize demonstrations. The demonstrations which occurred during the papal visit were an experience in self-government and revealed that the masses were capable of organizing their activities without the aid of government forces. Public opinion became animated and, although it was still fragmented, the level of agitation was significant. Political intimidation and lack of political experience within society still remained, however.

The second phase of the preliminary stage saw intellectual agitators joined by the more sensitive and politically conscious workers. The Committee for Free Trade Unions was also organized.

THE PRECIPITATION STAGE: SOCIETY AS A CROWD
(August 1980-November 1980)

This stage, marked by waves of strikes and an agreement between those in power and the labor class, was significant for later developments. The power elite's crisis of legitimacy became so apparent that the elite was virtually unable to dictate a hard-line solution to the striking labor class. Neither the surprising sacrifice of political scapegoats that occurred during the 8th Congress of the Communist Party nor the later, urgent reshuffling of the power elite satisfied the demands of the workers. The power elite was short of instrumental measures with which to exert political pressure. Until the summer of 1980 there was no democratic shift in power; the policies of the elite changed only when the internal coup occurred. Yet the level of determination and mobilization of the labor class exceeded the authorities' readiness to repress dissent by tough measures. The internal disorganization and disorientation of the ruling group explains its compromise on the agreement between itself and the workers. The agreement opened the door for the establishment of the trade union, and the subsequent wave of social enthusiasm and optimism brought the movement into legal existence. The fact that an agreement had been reached confirmed a general belief held by the Polish population that however serious conflicts might seem, there was always a possibility of settling them through negotiation.

The Communist Party, stripped of its top leadership, had to restructure its ranks. Two simultaneous moves occurred. First, the leaders of the moderate and pragmatic group were promoted to the governing bodies of the party. This process also reached the lower party ranks, where moderates suddenly appeared. Second, the group of hard-line politicians, long eliminated from the administration, found their way back into executive positions. Only the first of these processes was visible to the population.

The dominant form of social life in this period was the organized crowd. The belief that large numbers of people, gathered for specific purposes, could influence political decisions led the population to three erroneous assumptions: that the movement was omnipotent, that those in power would come to terms with society, and that the crisis could be overcome through spontaneous mobilization. The movement started to grow, even before its statement of purpose was made. By the end of this period the second and third waves of followers had joined the union, often defecting from the leading political party. This again promoted the notion that massive gatherings could influence political decision making.

Two distinct types of leaders emerged within the movement--the prophet and the activist. The prophetic leaders possessed charisma but no prior political experience. The activists, in contrast, usually presented some record of past political involvement, since they were usually recruited from the veterans of the 1956, 1968, 1970, and 1976 uprisings. These leaders were highly motivated toward collective action and, since they rejected compromise and governmental methods of wielding power, they promoted open discussion of critical issues. They believed that the overwhelming support for the movement was the result of national unity, although it actually resulted largely from the lack of alternative channels of opposition to the government. The optimism of this period was also evident in the general belief that the situation in Poland was unique. Several political and economic programs took this supposed uniqueness for granted (such as the DiP program and the early program outlined by Solidarity advisers).

THE POPULAR STAGE: SOCIETY AS EXCITED CROWD
(December 1980-March 1981)

Excitement, Unrest, and the Discovery of
Political Insincerity

This stage was marked by the formalization of the movement's existence. The leadership of the movement fell into the hands of intellectual advisers and enlightened workers who were fascinated by the logic of intellectual reasoning. New leaders, who favored reasoning over either political negotiations or making deals with the authorities emerged from among the young advisers. Subsequently, many reformers appeared in the lower levels of the movement's organization. The process of "setting the network" consisted of two activities. First, a vertical network was established to comply with the need for a hierarchical organization that could effectively negotiate with the authorities. Second, a horizontal network emerged spontaneously as the result of obstacles posed by the authorities. In a sense, the fact that the movement articulated the secondary, regional structure, which was later criticized for its radicalism, resulted from the two-faced politics of the authorities.

Since the horizontal structures were isolated from the decision-making process, they supplemented their knowledge with a conspiratorial vision of society and politics. Several commissions were formed within the movement to investigate cases of conspiracy. At the same time, however, the vertical structures rejected the arguments of alleged conspiracy; thus, the gap between the two networks widened. The masses were easily excited by scandals and rumors, which were rampant within the movement.

Yet another process characteristic of this stage was consistent agitation by intellectuals, which led to a period of discussion. The proportion of intelligentsia and white-collar workers in the movement grew rapidly. The effect of their socialization efforts was to raise the consciousness of the oppressed working class. The horizontal structures of the movement were especially vulnerable to persuasion through such means as hunger marches. The earlier belief that Poland was a uniquely successful country gave way to an extreme feeling that Poland was uniquely handicapped. But as a result of the rise in activity and political participation during this stage, individual political behavior was less marked by fear and intimidation.

THE DISORIENTATION STAGE: SOCIETY IN SEARCH
OF MEANING (March 1981-August 1981)

Polarization of Strategies

This stage was marked by the aggravation of the conflict between the movement and the political system, resulting in an increase of in-group consciousness. Following the compromise solution adopted during the crisis, several other cleavages appeared. Different opinions as to how the conflict should be settled led to a split in the leadership. This split was accompanied by two further steps. First, authoritarian methods were substituted for internal democracy within Solidarity, thereby lessening the likelihood of any realistic responses from the leadership. Second, both reformers and intellectuals experienced a weakening of their positions, while the prophetic elements of the leadership grew stronger. The increased role of charisma in the movement was accompanied by the tightening of links between the movement, the clergy, and the church bureaucracy. These links in turn encouraged the sacralization of the movement's practices. While this may have suited the majority of members, it certainly further weakened the role of rationality within the movement's pragmatic structures. The sacralization of the movement's practices was undoubtedly one of the reasons Solidarity was unable to recruit members from the existing power elite.

Several collective illusions grew in this period, contributing to the further disorientation of the masses. First was the belief in the continuing capacity of the Communist leadership to negotiate with the movement. Despite the apparent governmental inability to implement reforms, the belief spread that the movement could force authorities to do so, even without substantial structural changes within the management system. Second, was the assumption that the Catholic hierarchy in Poland would welcome the popular revolution. Third was the belief that the absence of external intervention meant that the authorities lacked the force necessary to suppress the movement. And last was the confidence that the movement could stay out of politics while formulating revolutionary demands which, if granted, would amount to the abdication of those in power.

THE DESTABILIZATION STAGE: PLURALIZED SOCIETY
(September 1981-December 1981)

Excitement, Fatigue, and Apathy

This stage began with the elaboration of the statement of objectives, purposes, and premises of the movement that were supposed to form a political credo. From this credo arose the body of criticism and condemnation of the existing social order. The leadership of the movement was still held by prophetic and charismatic personalities and only at a few local levels did more rational and effective leaders emerge. Some processes typical of social movements occurred during this period.

There were struggles among conservative, moderate, and radical factions in both the movement and the power elite. In addition, conflict and confrontation with the out-group continued, while class antagonism intensified. The moderate faction gained control in the movement, while the radical conservative faction assumed control in the power elite. Since the moderate reformers within the movement turned out to be just as incompetent as the reformers within the Party, the radicals of the movement made a coalition with conservatives in an attempt to seize power. The reformers were confronted by three handicaps: fear of armed invasion, fear of internal rebellion if they were unable to control the radicalized horizontal structures within the movement, and political inexperience. Moreover, the worsening of economic conditions and fatigue with everyday problems caused lukewarm supporters to desert; criticism of the movement increased. Lastly, patriotism, instead of joining with the "social myth" of Solidarity, became allied with Catholicism. The church further moderated the movement, forestalling a radical takeover and delaying confrontation with the government.

Several developments that might have transformed this period into the stage of formalization of the movement did not occur. First, the conservatives within the movement were not effectively eliminated since the fusion of patriotism and Catholicism blurred distinctions between the two. Second, the movement did not develop a defensive doctrine to back up its revolutionary, reformist objectives. Third, a gap widened between political rhetoric and the efficiency of policies, tactics, and practical operations. The movement did not concur in an ideology that would answer the unrest and discontent of the people. Finally, since the leadership was still in the hands of charismatic personalities who lost momentum following the compromise of March 1981, the radicals could not establish control. They did not seize power and the movement was unable to move forward.

THE TRUNCATION STAGE: THE MOVEMENT IN PIECES
(December 1981-May 1983)

Despair, Broken Hope, and Apathy

This stage was marked by the military takeover that suddenly wiped out the movement's legal structures. The introduction of terror and witch-hunting was intended to suppress activism, bring about widespread apathy, and produce a generalized belief in the overwhelming power of the new authorities. The disappearance of the movement's leaders was the first step in a long process of increasing apathy among the majority of members. Further attempts to truncate the movement failed when Solidarity rejected offers to join a coalition with the government; the governnment found it impossible to compromise the leaders or coopt a group of conformists who could dismantle the movement from within. In this light the crackdown appears as the most costly and dramatic attempt by the state to withdraw from earlier agreements. The disappearance of the leaders alone was not sufficient to truncate the movement effectively. People appeared to be committed to their beliefs, so that the removal of the leaders did not substantially weaken the movement. The government's next step was to introduce a reign of terror, making its power visible to all members of the society. The authorities counted on the psychological exhaustion of the masses to undermine the emotional foundations of the movement. Terror penetrated all areas of social life, depriving people of a sense of security in employment, in retirement, or in old age.

Several predictable processes occurred during this stage. The insecurity and ambiguity of the situation released such defensive mechanisms as resignation, withdrawal, and despair. When confronted by threats and danger to their dearest values, people turned to activities that offered immediate rewards. Escapist recreation, as well as the reemergence of graft, speculation, and corruption, appeared as symptoms of moral decline. The authorities made several attempts to launch waves of hostility, ethnocentrism, and isolationism among the masses. By differentially rewarding and punishing various categories, the government appeared to generate a significant amount of "internal emigration" of intellectuals from both the movement and other social institutions. The feeling of hopelessness was further deepened by the return of the old social structure. Despite these changes certain aspects of life continued to be shaped by the movement. Some institutional arrangements were retained and the intense interest of the average citizen in sociopolitical life remained undiminished.

THE RECONSTRUCTION STAGE: SOCIETY IN SEARCH OF A NEW MEANING (May 1983 -   )

Rebirth of Belief and Prudent Participation

This stage was marked by a rebirth of motivation, as well as the spreading belief that societal existence and dignity were at stake. People began to realize that there was nowhere else to go. Apparently, the authorities were unable to repress society completely because of its participation and belief in the movement. Actually, the truncation period contributed to the reconstruction period because of a series of vital strategic mistakes by those in power. Their major objective was to unveil the military might of the regime while maintaining a level of repression. As a consequence, two different policies unfolded.

Selected layers of society (the working class) were punished for participation but not for belief, which resulted in a tendency to withdraw temporarily from participation while still maintaining belief.

This kind of terror was characteristic of certain traditional dictatorships (Horthy, Salazar), which suppressed organized opposition, but were relatively unconcerned by private expressions of belief. These regimes ultimately failed.

Some other layers of society (intellectuals and white-collar workers) were punished for participation but rewarded for belief (because intrinsic mechanisms of social self-defense developed). Although participation declined, these groups retained their belief, which was further strengthened by the moral support of the environment. This environmental support is the reason why this group of people could not be recruited to such later movements as the "new" proregime union.

The second papal visit to Poland certainly contributed to the reconstruction stage. As the supreme moral authority, the pope supported Poles in their struggle for freedom. As during his 1979 visit, the pope stressed the political and moral dualism in Poland and opposed the societal values propounded in the rhetoric of those in power. The papal visit also catalyzed wide displays of support for Solidarity which, for obvious reasons, had not been seen since martial law was declared.

After a long period of enforced apathy Poles may again exhibit more specific political activities. Both sides in the conflict expect this to happen. From the government's point of view, the scenario would ideally include some minimal level of approval and legitimacy that would eliminate the most obvious strains, so that Poland would somehow return to the pre-Solidarity period, with people striving for individual affluence and the Communist Party governing. For the civil society, as run by the underground and pluralized opposition, the scenario would include a massive mobilization to paralyze the administrative structure of the Communist state and to revitalize Solidarity.

The first scenario is absolutely unrealistic and, although the authorities may experience short periods of relaxation, the population will never accept the legitimacy of its power. The second scenario is also unlikely to occur unless a popular revolution takes place to re-create the now truncated movement. Still the natural history of Solidarity is not yet over and the movement may be effectively truncated only for a short time. The movement may eventually disappear, but only after its major objectives have been realized (Sztompka 1982, 93).

Several situations might be conducive to the reappearance of the movement, namely:
1. Steered nationalism. In order to unify the society, authorities might provoke ethnocentric and nationalistic attitudes. If this nationalism becomes coupled with Catholicism,

it may provide a base for the "khomeinization" of the movement.
2. Enlightened Catholicism. Reinforced by the papal doctrine of seeking moral victory, Catholicism might effectively unify the society while undermining the Communist ideology. The "gandhization" of the movement would then be the outcome.
3. Socialist populism. The impoverishment of the working class might become so deep that it would be unbearable for rank-and-file Solidarity members. The ideology of "destatization" of socialism, as originated by Kuron and KOR, may spread, mobilizing the masses to create a communal organization. Obviously this would stimulate a Soviet response.
4. Intellectual democratism. Under a general collapse of the value system, intellectuals might initiate the action of "organic work." Short of experienced political cadres, the military regime might coopt intellectuals into the power elite, as they did in the 1970s. Some democratic concessions would have to be made just to extend the period of peace and to tranquilize the radicalism of the masses. In light of this radicalism, this could be only a temporary solution.

The Political Utility of Apathy and Participation

The future of Polish society is inseparable from the future of Solidarity, a movement born in misery, raised by hope, and buried by the political inexperience of members confronting the state apparatus too soon. It was in the immediate interest of the state to prevent people from participating and to extend the period of apathy and progressive deprivation that followed martial law. Apathy means not only the demobilization of the masses who, under the threat of the disruptive measures available to the state, refrain from strikes or street riots. Apathy also involves several psychological mechanisms, such as substitution, repression, and withdrawal. On the individual level these mechanisms may help people to survive the period of frustration of hope and privation of humanity; on the collective level they may account for the continuing ungovernability of Polish society.

The Freudian vision of society and politics is absolutely untenable at this point in time. A repressed individual is neither creative nor responsive. Such an individual may accept social coercion, sacrifice, and suffering, but is not likely to accept the changes and demands imposed by technology and the division of labor. Participation is not only a political activity, but also a way of life. It becomes a measure of social control when direct, coercive measures of control do not work. In this sense, participation means social maturity.

Subscribers to the Freudian vision may find it useful to have society immature, but no society can develop without the possibility of maturation. Poland can neither survive nor develop without channels for social participation. From a merely economic point of view one has to make people willing to work to improve their economic standing. The belief that the state in Poland could overcome or survive economic crises without societal cooperation is pure fantasy. If the period of apathy is extended beyond limits set by social psychology, the Polish economy will decline, the standard of living will deteriorate beyond tolerable limits, and the protracted conflict will result in another desperate outburst of spontaneous participation that could bring about further disillusionment. Apathy does not mean the absence of conflict, but only indicates the mood of a society paralyzed in its attempts to gain control over its own destiny. Protracted apathy and conflict would continue the vicious circle of collective behavior that further blocks chances for social participation and development. This is why the answer to the current stalemate in Poland has to be political rather than economic. Although it would be unreasonable to expect yet another revolution, extended apathy, unresolved conflicts, and repression of democracy limit Poland's socioeconomic development. The only viable alternative for the future of Poland is the return to participation.

REFERENCES

Albert, Michael and Robin Hahnel. 1981. Socialism Today and Tomorrow. Boston: South End Press.
Bauman, Zygmunt. 1971. "Twenty Years After: The Crisis of Soviet-type Systems." Problems of Communism 20 (November-December).
Blumer, Herbert. 1957. "Collective Behavior." in Joseph B. Gitter, ed. Review of Sociology: Analysis of a Decade. New York: John Wiley.
Davies, James C. 1962. "Toward a Theory of Revolution" American Sociological Review 27 (June).
Davies, Norman. 1982. God's Playground: A History of Poland. New York: Columbia University Press.
Farrel, Barry R. 1970. Political Leadership in Eastern Europe and the Soviet Union. Chicago: Aldine.
Gerlach, Luther P. 1971. "Movements of Revolutionary Change: Some Structural Characteristics." American Behavioral Scientists 14.
Hopper, Rex D. 1950. "The Revolutionary Process: A Frame of Reference for the Study of Revolutionary Movements." Social Forces 28 (March).
Karpinski, Jakub. 1981. Count-down: The Polish Upheavals of 1956, 1968, 1970, 1976, 1980.... New York: Karz-Cohl.
McLaughlin, Barry, ed. 1969. Studies in Social Movements: A Social Psychological Perspective. New York: Free Press.
Misztal, Barbara A., and Bronislaw Misztal. 1984. "Urban Social Problems in Poland. The macrosocial Determinants." Urban Affairs Quarterly 3.
Morrison, Denton E. 1971. "Some Notes Toward Theory on Relative Deprivation, Social Movements, and Social Change," American Behavioral Scientist 14.
Starski, Stanislaw. 1981. Class Struggle in Classless Poland. Boston: South End Press.
Steven, Stewart. 1982. The Poles. New York: Macmillan.
Szajkowski, Bogdan. 1983. Next to God· · · Poland. Boston: South End Press.
Sztompka, Piotr. 1982. "Dynamika ruchu odnowy w swietle teorii zachowania zbiorowego." Studia Socjologiczne 86-87.
Tucker, Robert C. 1976. "The Deradicalization of Marxist Movements." Robert H. Lauer, ed. Social Movements and Social Change. Carbondale: Southern Illinois University Press.
Weiss, Robert F. 1983. "Defection from Social Movements and Subsequent Recruitment to the New Movements." Sociometry 26 (March).

2
Solidarity and the State: Strategies of Social Reconstruction

Jack Bielasiak

Introduction

Explanations of the suppression of Solidarity by the State of War on December 13, 1981, focus on either the mistakes of Solidarity or the actions of the government. The controversy, which has been presented in scholarly and polemical evaluations, concerns the degree of responsibility borne by the two protagonists for the failure of the Solidarity experiment (Baker and Weber 1982; Staniszkis 1982b; de Weydenthal et al. 1983; Sanford 1983). The programs and activities of both the Solidarity movement and the Communist party-state are presented as two mirror images.
With regard to the independent trade union, a widespread argument is that the movement went too far to survive as a viable instrument for change in People's Poland. This view stresses the temporary politicization of Solidarity in 1980-1981 and the eventual radicalization of the movement. These features of the workers' organization are then presented as the reasons for the suppression of the labor union by the military regime. The leaders, advisers, and activists of the movement failed to exercise sufficient restraint and caution to assure the continuing acceptance of Solidarity as a social force in the Polish system.
Another image of Solidarity is at the polar extreme, arguing instead that labor's efforts were limited from the start and that the movement did not go far enough in its attempts to alter the Communist state. The focus here is on the assumption that from the very beginning Solidarity was subservient to the idea of reform and abandoned a revolutionary path to force change in Polish society (Barker and Weber 1982, 87-108). A better course would have been a commitment to a revolutionary stand that led to the reconstruction of Solidarity as a political party dedicated to the seizure of power by all means.
The course of action followed by the party-state is evaluated in similar analytical extremes. One view depicts the political apparatus as committed to the suppression of labor's autonomy from the beginning of

the workers' movement in August 1980. The subsequent "renewal" period was used by the party leadership to discredit Solidarity, to make the institutionalization of change difficult, and to obscure the deliberate preparations for the suppression of independent workers' power.

A different perception is held by observers who argue that the party-state was willing to absorb meaningful changes in the system of rule, as was evident in its tolerance of the labor movement in August 1980. This view stresses the willingness of the ruling elite to effect a reconciliation with the civil community through the intermediary of Solidarity. The failure of this good will was due to the labor movement's increasing politicization during the 1980-1981 period, forcing the party-state to abandon its "renewal" strategy of compromise. Instead the political authorities were forced to counteract Solidarity's push for power through recourse to coercive action.

This diversity of interpretations and the polemical rhetoric associated with it obscure the fundamental question with regard to the state-society relationship in Poland in 1980-1981. During that time the issue for both protagonists was whether and in what manner an independent working-class movement could be integrated within the social and political structure of state socialism. The problem was defined not only by the Polish United Workers' Party's (PUWP) claim to represent workers' interests, but also by the fact that the self-legitimacy of Communist rule depended on this presumption. To maintain the party-state's justification for political dominance over the entire society, the ruling party had to remain the embodiment of working-class consciousness. Solidarity's very existence was an assertion that such an arrangement did not adequately reflect the interests of the workers. The movement's insistence on alternative representation directly challenged the authority relations of state socialism.

The problem for the rulers and the ruled was to devise a formula that would satisfy both the Party's claim to rule in the name of the working class and Solidarity's claim to represent the genuine interests of industrial labor. Social stability, indeed the very survival of the nation, depended on the resolution of these competing concepts. The task for Solidarity and the regime was to create the necessary theoretical framework for the mutual coexistence of the Communist and the labor organizations and then to utilize the conceptual understanding to stabilize the state-society relationship in practice.

While the initial efforts of both sides were devoted to the resolution of this fundamental problem of representation and legitimacy, their respective understandings of the mutual agreement differed considerably. The solution was encapsulated in the social accords of August 31, 1980 (Protokoly 1980). This agreement between the Polish government and the Polish workers provided for the existence of an independent trade union within the political framework of state socialism and upheld the "leading role of the party" in the state. In their search for an acceptable accord, the regime and the labor movement were cognizant of historical constraints, practical limits, and political opportunities for the reconstruction of interactions between the state and the civil society. In their attempt to create this new form of existence, both sides were guided by their own theoretical approaches and conceptual understandings of the twenty-one agreements. The tragedy for Poland was that these interpretations were fundamentally at odds and contributed to the evolving misunderstanding between the two protagonists. The final result was to force the regime and Solidarity into a pattern of behavior that aggravated social instability and ultimately led to an irreconcilable schism between the state and society.

From Limits to Theories of Reconstruction

After August 1980 the primary task for the party authorities and the Solidarity leadership involved the formation of a social structure capable of accommodating the party and labor organizations in a completely politicized system. In practice, the institutionalization of workers' interests outside the Communist party depended on coming to terms with the monopoly of political power claimed by the party-state apparatus. The articulation and implementation of a program safeguarding the "leading role of the party" principle and facilitating the formation of an autonomous workers' organization were severely constrained by historical, geopolitical, and theoretical limits. In combination, these factors defined the search for a conceptual and practical solution to the coexistence of the state and civil society (Solidarnosc 1980; Kowalik 1983). While both the PUWP and Solidarity leaders were well aware of the operating limits, the content within these boundaries varied for each side.

The limits

From the perspective of Solidarity, its challenge to the status quo was restricted by environmental and theoretical constraints. The former dealt essentially with restrictions on the overt pursuit of political power by the labor movement. The limits were defined in the first instance by the hegemony of Soviet interests in the region, involving security concerns and ideological principles. The overriding demands of the Soviet ruling elite centered on the inviolability of the socialist alliance system and on the primacy of the Communist party in the domestic relations of the East European states. From a historical perspective, these limits on change in the socialist community were definitively established by events surrounding the Hungarian Revolution of 1956 (Tatu 1981; Vali 1961). The uprising in Budapest not only made clear the <u>sine qua non</u> of withdrawal from the Warsaw Pact and of the destruction of the ruling party, but also disqualified a revolutionary mass uprising as an instrument of change in state socialism. The Hungarian "revolution from below" could not be an operational model for Solidarity without risking immediate suppression.

While historical lessons had a practical effect on the posture of Solidarity, the workers' organization was also confined in its program by theoretical principles that defined the social behavior of the new movement. From its very creation Solidarity embodied a dedication to openness, truth, and democracy that contrasted sharply with the environment established by the party-state (Pomian 1982). It was precisely these aspects that attracted considerable popular support for Solidarity, manifested by a rapid rise in its membership and the emulation of the movement by other sectors of society. From the very beginning, therefore, Solidarity represented the popular will of society. While this was of course a significant source of strength, the position ascribed to Solidarity by the civil community also presented considerable danger. By its dedication to social autonomy and the self-organization of social groups, Solidarity had attained a growing hegemony over the consciousness of society (for the concept, see Gramsci 1973, 1978). The translation of its hegemonic influence from the realm of popular consciousness to the sphere of political reality presented the danger of transforming the movement from a new type of social force into an old-line political party. Moreover, such a transformation held out the possibility of a Leninist process whereby Solidarity could emerge as an organized political force representing the entire civil society. Solidarity in such a case would become the new vanguard of society, displacing the ruling Communist party. The formation of a political hegemonic relationship toward society was also likely to create Leninist forms of organization, turning the movement away from its open, self-governing features to authoritarian and hierarchical modes of behavior. This transformation of Solidarity was a real possibility, had the movement embarked on a deliberate political strategy from its very inception. The commitment of Solidarity members and activists to a new form of organization precluded the movement's assumption of political control over the rest of society. In this sense a self-limitation was operating over the strategy assumed by Solidarity, based on the rejection of a Leninist theoretical solution to the problem of power in a state in crisis.

Similar practical and theoretical considerations played a role in the determination of the regime's response to the formation of the Solidarity movement. From a practical standpoint, the process of change initiated by the striking workers in the summer of 1980 had to be limited to a sphere external to the party and its operational ability to pursue a commanding function in the system. The reality of these constraints was defined for the party establishment by the political experience of the 1968 Prague Spring (Skilling 1976; Valenta 1979). Just as the Hungarian Revolution represented a historically defined boundary for the policies and actions of the Solidarity movement, so the Czechoslovak events informed the political course of the Polish Communist regime in 1980. In this instance, the example touched on the immunity of the ruling Communist organization to the reformist trends prevalent in society. In the eyes of international Communism, the principal failure of the Prague Spring was the transformation of the party into a reformist organ initiating changes throughout the system.

In the aftermath of the Warsaw Pact intervention in Czechoslovakia, it became clear that the assumption of a revisionist stand by a ruling Communist party went beyond the limits of tolerance. At stake, from the point of view of Soviet interests, was the ability of the ruling party to maintain authority and control. The "leading role of the party" was interpreted not as a source of redefinition for the state-society relationship but as an embodiment of the vanguard role of the party in formulating the process of social development (Kania 1980a, 1980b). The practical determination for this criterion was the propensity of the ruling Communist bodies to supervise (and intervene in case of need) in political decision making, economic management, and the administration of society. While the civil community could exercise an influence in these processes, the ultimate arbiter was to remain the Communist party. For the Polish regime, the task in the face of the formation of Solidarity and the autonomous organization of other groups was to formulate a policy that would contain these newly awakened forces.

The primary motivation of the Polish leadership was to prevent a repetition of the Czechoslovak scenario of 1968. This goal was strongly reinforced by theoretical considerations that placed the leading role of the party at the very foundation of the Polish political system. The claim to political rule on the part of the Communist elite rested on the ideological definition of the party as representing the consciousness of society and as providing the ruling strata with the justification to act as the vanguard for the entire society. Without the embodiment of this consciousness, the party could not maintain its dominant position in the system. In a very real sense, the Leninist formulation established the theoretical form of the Communist state. Reformist concepts that diluted the Communist organization's role undermined the very nature of state socialism. For that reason, the issue of the "leading role of the party" went far beyond the party's ability to direct state and mass organizations. In fact, while the Communist party could tolerate an erosion of its practical hold over society, it could not accept the theoretical rejection of its leading role in the system. The articulation of a policy of renewal in the aftermath of the August events revised the content of the principle without altering its essential meaning.

The solutions

The theoretical and practical constraints imposed on the evolution of Solidarity and the strategy of the party-state defined the range of solutions to the problem of coexistence. The basic response was to distinguish between the state and society as separate spheres of social interaction. The defining concept (Staniszkis 1981b)--the "self-limiting revolution"--of Solidarity's challenge to the existing conditions not only recognized this distinction, but also placed it at the forefront of the union's program. Although the ruling party did not overtly admit to the separation of society from the state, it did acknowledge the utility of such a division by accepting the workers' recognition in the Gdansk accords of the PUWP's "leading role in the state" (Protokoly, 2). While clearly identifying the dominant role of the Communist party, the formulation confined that function to a narrower arena of activity.
Solidarity's principle of the self-limiting revolution and the regime's acceptance of the party's leading role in the state created the essential formula for the separation of society from the state and by this means provided an opportunity for changing the relationship between the party-state and the civil community. Interestingly, the distinction between the political and civil spheres had been the program of the Polish dissident movement in the late 1970s. In their search for a viable strategy for altering the Communist system in Poland, dissidents had to take into account the failures of the Hungarian "revolution from below" and the Czechoslovak "reform from above." The program devised by the democratic opposition was that of the new evolutionism, relying on a strategy of change

through "reform from below" (Michnik 1976; Kuron 1978). The fundamental premise of the new evolutionism was that change in state socialism could be achieved only by dissociating society from the state. The task involved a gradual process of separating the functions of organized political power (to remain in the form of the state) and that of the civil community (to be organized in independent associations). This necessitated first of all the reconstruction of the civil society under state socialism. The only possibility for the successful evolution of separate official and public spheres rested with intiatives from below by society. Social forces had to organize and openly present their demands for transforming the system of power and for establishing a more equal relationship between the state and civil society. The aim was to facilitate actions by social groups that would foster the reemergence of the civil community. This took the form of creating an atmosphere of open discourse through appeals to constitutional civil rights and legal conduct. Such actions served a dual purpose, first by creating a freer public sphere and second by establishing restraints on the political power of the socialist institutions.

The advantage of the new evolutionism was that it sought to change social patterns without attempting to seize state power. Rather the program called for the self-organization of society through the formation of autonomous associations representing diverse interests and acting as social self-defense mechanisms vis-a-vis organized political power. The hope was that this type of confrontation of the ruling establishment by society would redefine the structure of state socialism without providing the party-state with the opportunity to suppress civil society.

The emergence of the workers' movement in the summer of 1980 and the regime's response in August confirmed the expectations of new evolutionism (Ascherson 1981; Bielasiak and Simon 1984). The challenge of the working class to state socialism precluded the seizure of political power as a result of the theoretical and practical self-limits constraining Solidarity. The labor union's willingness to confine its activity in turn enabled the party-state to accept the distinction between two separate spheres of activity--a politicized sector and one confined to the civil interests of society.

The disengagement of the civil society from state power was the essential feature in the theoretical solution to the dilemma of the PUWP and Solidarity's coexistence. While providing the answer in principle, the state-civil society distinction did not resolve in practice the issue of the respective competencies and institutional prerogatives of the party and Solidarity organizations. There were in fact three possible forms of the redefined state-society relationship (Kuron 1981b; Michnik 1981; Staniszkis 1982; Dubet et al. 1982; Arato 1981).

The first possibility concerned the actual depoliticization of civil society. In this concept society was to be nonpolitical, in the sense of abstaining from exercising power or making authoritative decisions. Rather society was to be composed of independent organizations representing various social groups and acting on their behalf with the state. This system was to function through the particularization of state-society interactions, with each autonomous association dealing separately with the authorities. The civil society would exercise influence in, and restraint over, policies without assuming responsibility for governing.

A second option involved the coexistence of political spheres in both the state and society. The arrangement would come closer to a duality of power through the formation of a more organized and integrated civil society operating in the realm of policy making alongside the party-state. The sharing of decision-making prerogatives was to be regulated by institutionalized interactions in the form of negotiations, bargaining, and compromise. Stability would be assured through regularized access to the procedures of governing, as well as through voluntary self-limitation on the part of the two partners.

The third solution centered on the depoliticization of the state. In this case, civil society was to determine policy, while the state implemented and administered decisions. This role for the civil society did not necessarily mean the transformation of Solidarity into a political party. Rather the formation of multiple social movements--of workers, peasants, students, and professionals--was viewed as leading to the self-management of society. The process would provide the civil society with self-rule while effectively limiting the tasks of the party-state, which would assume administrative functions to implement the decisions of the self-governing society.

Theoretically all three scenarios--the depoliticized society, shared political power, and the depoliticized state--satisfied the constraints on the reconstruction of state socialism. In reality, however, the implementation of the state-society distinction favored the first solution. The awareness of historical precedents, geopolitical limits, and theoretical concerns predisposed Solidarity's self-limiting revolution toward the recreation of civil society based on the depoliticized model. Yet this initial choice was not the exclusive solution to the problem of coexistence between the Communist and labor organizations. The other forms of the self-limiting challenge to the party-state remained possible alternatives to the transformation of state socialism. The reality of the Polish political situation in the aftermath of the August Agreements in fact led to redefinitions of the process of change adopted by Solidarity. These choices were dictated by the dynamics of power politics during the course of 1980-1981, and were alternately spontaneous or deliberate adjustments to the policies and actions of the party-state. These alterations in turn stimulated further changes on the part of the Communist apparatus and its definition of the acceptable program of social reconstruction (Bielasiak 1984). The interactions among these diverse policies and activities of the two protagonists imposed a move toward other theoretical scenarios for the organization of society and polity.

Solidarity and the Praxis of Reconstruction

Solidarity's attempt to alter the structure of state socialism can be divided into three strategic phases. While it is important to recognize that the boundaries between the diverse approaches are blurred, that certain features of Solidarity's program transcended any particular phase, that there were substantive differences in Solidarity throughout its existence, distinct concepts and strategic choices nonetheless dominated each stage of the union's evolution.

The trade-unionist phase

The first stage in Solidarity's attempt to alter the Polish reality took the form of emphasizing the trade-unionist nature of the labor movement. From the formation of the Interfactory Strike Committees (MKS) in the summer through the registration crisis of November 1980, the self-identification of Solidarity was as an organization representing the working class against the political and managerial power of the party-state (interviews with Solidarity leaders, Polityka, October 18, 1980 and November 1, 1980; Kuron 1981a). The theoretical assumptions centered on the nonpolitical aspects and aspirations of the movement and avoided the temptation to seize and exercise power. In many ways this posture was characterized by a deliberate political disengagement on the part of Solidarity leaders, who sought instead to contain the workers' organization within the trade-unionist formula. Lech Walesa repeatedly stressed at the time that "we are trade unions and only trade unions," without political ambitions (in Robinson 1980, 435).

The political territory was consciously conceded to the Communist party, while Solidarity's efforts to transform social existence concentrated on the restoration of civil society. In this task the workers were motivated by the corruption of the political sector in Poland, which alienated the population from participation in political life. Interactions with the ruling establishment on the political plane thus signified descent into an arena that had become abhorent to the working class. Labor's resistance to political intercourse and responsibility for policy stemmed from these intuitive realities (Bauman 1981). Worker activists preferred to engage their efforts in the creation of a civil community subject to new values and new rules.

For that reason, the idea of civil society became synonymous with commitments to democratic and truthful forms of association. These values, together with the outpouring of working-class solidarity, defined the establishment of a public sphere independent of state power and governed by its own "apolitical" forms. The exercise of political power had a corrupting effect that was best avoided. Rather than being drawn into the official process, Solidarity preferred to alter it by imposing external limits on the application of power in the civil society.

The aim was not to conquer the state but to reform its interaction with society. The method was the formation of a civil society in which diverse social forces were organized into independent associations. The latter's tasks were to provide genuine representation to different social groups and to intervene with the ruling apparatus in the interests of society. While both group and societal representations had a natural place in the reconstructed civil society, the primary function of each autonomous organization was to act in the name and on behalf of its constituents. In this self-defined view Solidarity was primarily a union representing the industrial workers of Poland. This symbiotic relationship did not mean the abandonment of the civil society as a whole, for the well-being of the labor union depended on the existence and functioning of other similarly organized social strata. The presence of such autonomous and democratic institutions defined the civil society and safeguarded its vitality from the party-state.

The public sphere was characterized by a pluralism of interests, while organized political power remained the province of the ruling Communist party. The authority of the party-state, however, was circumscribed by the newly autonomous social groups, which constrained the ruling establishment by guarding their members' interests. In the view of Solidarity, this retrenchment of political power was symbolized by the formula of the leading role of the party in the state, not in society. The significance of the redefinition was not only that the interventionist capabilities of the apparatus in society were limited, but also that the ruling elite retained responsibility for policy formulation and implementation. As a trade-union, Solidarity rejected coresponsibility for governing. This stance was advantageous in that it did not assume political accountability by the trade-union but placed a constraining force on the authority of the Communist party.

The mechanism of social transformation was the regularized process of interaction between autonomous social groups and the party-state. Prior to the restoration of civil society, the ruling party had the capacity to impose its preferences on a defenseless public. The emergence of independent groupings throughout the civil society precluded such a political pattern. Rather, on issues of concern to the diverse organizations, the ruling apparatus had to contend with the opinions and preferences of society. While the public did not make policy, it acted "from below" to define the program's acceptability to social forces. The interactions between the party-state and the civil society over a range of particularized issues determined the content of the government's economic and social policy. Most importantly, the introduction and recognition of regularized procedures for the state-society dialogue created a new structure in state socialism, effectively altering the Communist system of power.

In the final analysis, Solidarity's trade-unionist strategy depended on the institutionalization and regularization of the dialogue between the state and society. This approach relied on the implementation of a novel process of interaction between the rulers and the ruled. While substance was of concern, it was not as critical to the definition of a reconstructed relationship between the party-state and the civil society as provisions for access by social organizations to the centers of political decision making. The establishment of an independent workers' organization with guarantees of autonomy through the right to strike and freer means of expression were paramount in this phase of Solidarity's development. Procedural mechanisms were the means through which civil society would shape policy content.

The politicization phase

The success of the trade-unionist concept in transforming the state-society relationship depended on the institutionalization of procedural innovations between the ruling establishment and Solidarity. The latter's understanding of the Gdansk Agreements and its willingness to adhere to a limited strategy of reform centered on the belief that the new freedoms and the movement's strength were sufficient to impose a program of reconstruction on the party-state. While the signing of the Gdansk Agreements by the government was taken as a formal recognition of this development, guarantees for the evolution of change were the autonomy of social organizations and their right to the expression of public interests.
The party-state's attempt to erode these independent guarantees produced the first major crisis in the post-August relationship between the ruling circles and civil society. The consequence was a shift in November 1980 away from the theoretical emphasis on trade-unionism and the initiation of a transitional phase of mobilization through the winter and spring of 1980-1981.
The precipitating factor in the conceptual alteration of Solidarity's posture was the official attempt to redefine the union's position at the time of its registration as an independent national organization (Ascherson 1981). The government's actions involved the unilateral insertion of a clause in Solidarity's statutes, asserting that the movement recognized the Communist party's leading role. The move was perceived as an attempt to circumscribe the autonomy of the union, for recognition of the party's primacy was to be shifted from a protocol between the state and society, as in August, to the internal functioning of the labor organization. From the perspective of the regime, this signified a simple commitment on the part of Solidarity to the socialist system. From the viewpoint of the workers, the move placed Solidarity's own structure under the auspices of state power. The internalization of the leading role of the party also incorporated the trade-union into official political rules, drawing Solidarity into political sphere on terms defined by the regime. This was the first step in a pattern evident after the 1956 and 1970 crises: the cooptation of autonomous social forces into the existing political reality of state socialism (Bielasiak 1984). It was precisely what the workers had rejected during the August confrontations. Only the threat of a general strike succeeded in altering the government's position and in concluding a compromise.
The regime's interference in Solidarity's bylaws was symptomatic of the failures to establish regular-

ized, mutually accommodating processes of state-society interactions. The party-state sought to extend its own political values and processes into the civil society, or, failing that, to retreat into inaction and isolation. As a result, the governing apparatus abdicated the responsibility to rule. Social forces had to turn to strikes to repulse the interventionist forays of the regime into the civil society or to assure policy fulfillment by the authorities. The consequence was the escalation of confrontations between society and the state.

Solidarity's trade-union concept proved too narrow to form a new pattern of party-community relations. Such an approach placed the autonomous social forces into a reactive mode of behavior vis-a-vis the state, without providing sufficient procedural resources to influence the regime. This led to the reinterpretation of Solidarity's theoretical and practical positions toward the dilemma of Communist and labor organizations' coexistence, a development fostered by the growing deterioration of social conditions and the increasing discontent of grass-roots forces.

Mobilization for a new posture produced at first tentative results, but nonetheless shifted Solidarity's approach away from the depoliticization of society to a duality of political sectors in the state and the civil society. Definitional aspects began to focus on Solidarity as a working-class movement embodying the very idea of society (Directions of Solidarity 1981). The labor organization was without question the strongest element in the public sector; its existence allowed the formation of other independent social groups. The responsibility thus placed on Solidarity reinforced the image of the union as the corporate body of the civil society. The view implied that society could be organized as an integrated force capable of interacting on an equal footing with the party-state. The former perception of particularized linkages between discrete social units and the government gave way to the view of equal partners interacting on the basis of an established social contract. The Gdansk Agreements, as that contract, delineated the respective areas of activity for the party-state and the civil society and imposed on each side defined areas of social responsibility.

The above definitions still maintained the separation of practices prevailing in the public and official spheres. Society's re-creation of a pluralist and democratic process persevered alongside the monolithic and authoritarian structure of the party-state. Contractual obligations fostered society's nonintervention in the practices of the Communist party and the latter refrained from altering the civil society (Geremek 1981a, 1981b). To assure the arrangement, the political dialogue between the two protagonists involved an equal relationship and concerned the content of the social contract. Solidarity was willing to assume a more extensive role as a partner with defined areas of social responsibility, providing it with a place in policy formation and implementation. Such an arrangement, it was hoped, would prevent official inactivity from neglecting societal interests. Furthermore, the interactions between the PUWP and Solidarity would concern the very content of the agreements between the state and society. Negotiations and bargaining, in this vision of political dualism, had a direct influence on the content of the contractual arrangement. In this instance, the reform of state socialism depended not only on procedural checks on government action by autonomous social organizations but also on the specific policy arrangements concluded in the negotiation sessions.

The renovation of the state-society relationship was thus the coresponsibility of the official and public sectors; it was also the function of both procedural access by independent institutions to policy areas and the negotiated content of the reformulated social contract. The movement in Solidarity's position was the consequence of the growing awareness that procedural guarantees of institutional autonomy and strike action were insufficient resources for the determination of the country's social and economic program. The substance of policy could not be left to the province of the party-state apparatus; measures assuring society's role in the formulation of substantive policy had to be created. This need formed the pressures for the assumption of a politicized role by Solidarity. However reluctant the movement's leaders were in succumbing to such a transformation, the position, delay, and inaction of the party-state increasingly formed the conditions for the politicization of the workers' organization.

The social movement phase

The evolution of Solidarity toward a position of dual political responsibility was interpreted by the party-state as the effective interpenetration of the civil and political sectors in the Polish system. The cross-membership between the two organizations, the growth of the horizontal movement within the party, and the gradual devolution of party-state functions throughout the spring of 1981 were taken as concrete manifestations of the interlinking of the public and official spheres. The development of these phenomena strengthened the ruling establishment in the position of maintaining control over the state structure.

The regime's fear, strongly reinforced by voices from the socialist community, was that the dominant role of the Communist organization, even within a narrow, official framework, could not be maintained in the face of the theoretical and practical alterations in the state-society relationship. The reaction of the power elite was to contain the widening role of the workers' organization. The Bydgoszcz incident in late March 1981 was a preliminary foray in that direction. The reaction took a milder form during the spring but was reinforced again by the June letter from the Soviet leaders to their Polish counterparts (Trybuna Ludu, June 11, 1981). The crowning of this antagonistic position occurred in mid-July at the Ninth Extraordinary PUWP Congress, whose relatively open process masked the reassertion of the political apparatus and the lack of substantive programs for the resolution of the nation's problems (Trybuna Ludu, July 15, 16, 17, 18, 19, and 20, 1981).

The stalemate in the program and the shift in the official power configuration rendered inoperative Solidarity's "dual politics" strategy, for the potential partner defined itself as an adversary. The strike weapon and a forced bargaining process were insufficiently productive mechanisms for the resolution of the problems facing society. Solidarity had to engage in a more positive involvement in policy determination to reconstruct the social conditions. The precipitating factors in shifting Solidarity's strategy once again were the increasing frustration and activism of grass-roots elements within the movement. The process began in the spring with the articulation of alternatives, such as the self-management program of the Network of Leading Enterprises (Siec 1981). It then led to the overt expression of public discontent in the summer, through hunger marches and street demonstrations, and culminated in the proclamation of a new program at the first Congress of Solidarity in September 1981.

The result was the overt recognition of Solidarity as a social movement representing the aspirations of the entire nation. While the tendency to view the labor organization in those terms was present from the beginning of the August events, the articulation of the concept was eschewed as too extreme to enable the transformation of state socialism. The force of circumstances finally reasserted the social movement formulation into the forefront of union activity, but the problems associated with it remained. The primary danger still concerned Solidarity's assumption of a hegemonic position in society, effectively displacing the Communist party from its vanguard role in any sphere of social or political activity. The attendant realpolitik implications for the functioning of state socialism were obvious. Equally significant was the potential of Solidarity's succumbing to the Leninist impulse by replacing the ruling party's dominance with its own. The severity of both problems found expression in the increasing tensions among the movement's leaders, advisers, and activists, concerning Solidarity's role, goals, and methods (Gwiazda 1982; Walesa 1982). Intraorganizational divisions began to predominate and secretive, hierarchical, disciplinary Leninist tendencies were reinforced. Mass pressure and the intransigence of the regime nonetheless culminated in Solidarity's articulation of the third strategy of change. The movement had to assume a more politicized posture to succeed in its tasks. The new concept focused on Solidarity as a broad social movement embodying the civil society. The labor association's concerns were no longer defined as economic power relations between the state and the working class, but embraced the entire spectrum of social, economic, cultural, and political relations between the party-state and civil society. In this manner, the responsibility of Solidarity now extended into the political arena as the representative of the entire community. Its function was to provide civil society with an initiating role in the political process, in contrast with its prior emphasis on reactive and bargaining roles.

The responsibility involved first the formation of institutional arrangements assuring the labor organization's participation in policy formation and execution (Walesa 1981). The theoretical construct thus stressed the formation of a self-governing civil society, defined by self-management structures at all levels and in all spheres of socioeconomic activity (<u>Program NSZZ Solidarnosc</u> 1981). The idea was to create a society capable of initiating action and of assuring the propagation of policy innovation to solve the outstanding economic and social problems of the nation. Enterprise and neighborhood self-management schemes were to establish workers' and citizen's control over the basic functions of social life in Poland. The trend would lead to the formation of a self-governing republic, including a chamber of self-management organizations in the Polish parliament.

The endorsement of self-governing programs by Solidarity was a reaction to its previous failures to assure the civil society of powers of representation and the protection of its economic and social interests. The participatory schemes signified the assumption of increased responsibility for the economy and society, in effect creating the self-rule of society. The practical abdication of policy responsibility by the political establishment justified, from the movement's perspective, the depoliticization of the state. The party-state was to be reduced to an administrative apparatus concerned foremost with the execution of directives stemming from the self-governing civil society. The political functions of policy making and agenda setting were to revert from the official--but now dormant--structures to the public sphere. Self-management presented the additional advantage of facilitating the expression of a plurality of interests coexisting in society, without dominance by Leninist-type organizations in the guise of Communist or Solidarity power. The self-ruling community was to be a safeguard against a renewed hegemonization and subservience of civil society to a political force external to the public sphere.

Self-management, however, was not to be exclusively a procedural innovation. Rather the concept of self-government encapsulated in the social movement theory reverted to the original "new evolutionism" view that the self-organization of society was an essential component of the reconstructed system of Communist power. Self-government was part of the substantive rearrangement of state socialism, holding a prominent place alongside the other values expressed by Solidarity. In the final analysis, change in the system of rule could not be left to the uncertain dynamics of political and social processes, but had to be guaranteed by a fundamentalist restructuring of society. Fundamentalism meant above all dedication to the values of nation, democracy, freedom, equality, and justice found in the civil society. The depoliticization of the state and the assumption of governance by the civil society provided for the introduction of these principles into the political sector. Ultimately, the open social movement phase of Solidarity was directed at upholding the content of the movement, expressed in its ideals and policies, over the concern with changes in the procedural interactions between the state and society.

Conclusion

The history of Solidarity reveals considerable awareness on the movement's part of its responsibilities to society. In the initial phase of its existence, the labor organization's concerns were directed toward altering state socialism within the limits imposed by realpolitik and theoretical considerations. Revolutionary action aimed at the seizure of state power was not only precluded by geopolitical realities, but also held out the potential of the movement's transformation from representation to domination of civil society. The preferred course was to adopt the principle of the "self-limiting revolution" as a conscious effort to forestall either eventuality. The chosen method was to work through "reform from below" to reconstruct civil society alongside a renewed party-state.

The initial manifestations of the attempt turned to a trade-unionist concept of the Solidarity movement that proved too narrow to assure the reconstruction of the party-state. The initiative met with the ruling elite's refusal to accept a reformulated "leading role of the party" principle as the means to change the Communist system. Instead, official delays and obstacles precluded the stabilization of coexistence between the state and civil society, between the party and Solidarity.

The evolution of Solidarity to more politicized forms of expression occurred as a consequence of the environment of inaction established by the regime. Solidarity's responsibility to the civil society included the resolution of the economic and social problems prevalent in the country. To assure regularized inputs into policy making, Solidarity had to institutionalize the process of change. This meant the abandonment of a forced trade-unionist concept and the ultimate self-acceptance of Solidarity as a social movement of national dimensions. The resultant expansion of Solidarity's political aspirations was aimed at creating and influencing a program of social, economic, and political reconstruction in Poland. Solidarity's attempts to expand its influence in society and polity diminished further the party's "leading role" prerogatives. To forestall what it viewed as the transformation of the Leninist system, the party-state was reduced to reestablishing its control by the use of force. Paradoxically, the defense of the leading role of the party had to rely on a military instrument that used a new language and new structures to preserve the Leninist form of the party-state.

The State of War nonetheless made clear that the state-organized political power controlled the instruments of force despite the growing hegemony of Solidarity in the community. The theoretical disintegration of party hegemony in the system ultimately forced the ruling elite to reach for coercive action to assure the state's dominance over society. In contrast, the weakness of Solidarity's "self-limiting revolution" rested with its inability to institutionalize the new vision of the reconstructed state-society structure. That failure stemmed from the conscious effort to avoid the Leninist impulse of gaining control of state power at all costs, including the ideals of the movement. The value of the self-limiting revolution was in Solidarity's commitment to the preservation of civil society and its ideals, and in the denial of state hegemony and its power.

REFERENCES

Arato, Andrew. 1981. "Civil Society Against the State: Poland 1980-1981." Telos 47 (Spring).
Ascherson, Neal. 1981. The Polish August. New York: Penguin.
Barker, Colin and Kara Weber. 1982. Solidarnosc From Gdansk to Military Repression. London: International Socialism.
Bauman, Zygmunt. 1981. "On the Maturation of Socialism." Telos 47 (Spring).
Bielasiak, Jack and Maurice Simon, eds. 1984. Polish Politics: Edge of the Abyss. New York: Praeger.
de Weydenthal, Jan B., Bruce D. Porter, and Kevin Devlin. 1983. The Polish Drama: 1980-1982. Lexington, Mass.: Lexington Books.
Directions of the Operations of the Independent, Self-Governing Trade Union Solidarity in the Current Situation of the Country. 1981. Tygodnik Solidarnosc (April 17, in Polish).
Dubet, Francois, Alain Touraine and Michel Wiewiorka. 1982. "A Social Movement: Solidarity." Telos 53 (Fall).
Geremek, Bronislaw. 1981a. Interview. Kurier Polski (November 27-29).
_____. 1981b. Interview. Polityka (August 8).
Gramsci, Antonio. 1978. Selections from Political Writings. New York: International Publishers.
_____. 1973. Letters From Prison. New York: Harper and Row.
Gwiazda, Andrzej. 1982. "Open Letter." Stan Persky and Henry Flam, eds. The Solidarity Sourcebook Vancouver: New Star Books.
Kania, Stanislaw. 1980a. Speech at the VI Plenum of the PUWP Central Committee.Trybuna Ludu (November 8, in Polish).
_____. 1980b. Speech to the PUWP actif in Gdansk, Ideologia i Polityka 11 (November, in Polish).
Kowalik, Tadeusz. 1983. "Proba Kompromisu." Zeszyty Literackie 2 (Spring).
Kuron, Jacek. 1981a. "Un Chemin sans Retour." Esprit 1 (January).
_____. 1981b. "What Next in Poland." Dissent (Winter).
_____. 1978. Zasady Ideowe. Paris: Instytut Literacki (in Polish).
Michnik, Adam. 1981. "What We Want to Do and What We Can Do" Telos 47 (Spring).
_____. 1976. "The New Evolutionism." Survey 22 (3/4, Summer-Autumn).
Polityka. 1980. October 18 and November 1.

Pomian, Grazyna. 1982. Polska "Solidarnosci". Paris: Instytut Literacki (in Polish).
Program NSZZ Solidarnosc. 1981. Tygodnik Solidarnosc (October 16, in Polish).
Protokoly Porozumien Gdansk, Szczecin, Jastrzebie. 1980. Warsaw: KAW (in Polish).
Robinson, William F. 1980. August 1980: The Strikes in Poland. Munich: Radio Free Europe Research.
Sanford, George. 1983. Polish Communism in Crisis. London: Croom Helm.
Siec Wiodacych Zakladow Pracy. 1981. "Dokumenty i Opracowania." NTO. 8 (July).
Skilling, H. Gordon. 1976. Czechoslovak Interrupted Revolution. Princeton, N. J.: Princeton University Press.
Solidarnosc: Strajkowy Biuletyn Informacyjny Gdansk. 1980. No. 1 (August 23) to No. 13 (August 31).
Staniszkis, Jadwiga. 1982a. "Polish Peaceful Revolution: An Anatomy of Polarization. Journal of Peace Research 19 (no. 2).
_____ 1982b. Pologne: La Revolution Autolimitee. Paris: Presses Universitaires de France.
_____ 1981a. "The Evolution of Forms of Working Class Protest in Poland: Sociological Reflections on the Gdansk-Szczecin Case, August 1980," Soviet Studies 33 (April).
_____ 1981b. "Samoograniczajaca Sie Rewolucja." Kultura (March 22, in Polish).
Tatu, Michel. 1981. "Intervention in Eastern Europe." Diplomacy of Power. Stephen S. Kaplan, ed. Washington, D. C.: Brookings Institution.
Trybuna Ludu. 1981. June 11 and July 15, 16, 17, 18, 19, and 20.
Valenta, Jiri. 1979. Soviet Intervention in Czechoslovakia 1968. Baltimore: Johns Hopkins University Press.
Vali, Fareno A, 1961. Rift and Revolt in Hungary. Cambridge, Mass.: Harvard University Press.
Walesa, Lech. 1982. "Reply to the Open Letter." Stan Persky and Henry Flam, eds. The Solidarity Sourcebook. Vancouver: New Star Books.
_____ 1981. Interview. Polityka (October 17, in Polish).

3
Institutionalization of the Party-State Regime in Poland

Paul G. Lewis

The party-state whose origins lay in the Russian upheavals of 1917 could not fail to be influenced by the particular relationship between state and society in prerevolutionary Russia. The evolution of Russian society has long been marked by the strong, if not suffocating, influence of the state and its centralized apparatus. While the classic Marxian view of revolution alludes to the supercession of the state by the forces of developed capitalist society, notably the proletariat, the origins of the Soviet party-state owe more to the particular circumstances provided by Russian history. The spontaneous action of social forces (e.g. workers afflicted with a "trade union" consciousness) was consistently criticized by Lenin; the embryo of the later party-state was clearly to be seen in his prerevolutionary writings. The Marxian vision of the state being superceded by mature social forces has not been enacted in the Russian experience.

Nevertheless, the party-state established and developed after the Russian Revolution was no mere extension of the tsarist edifice. It learned and developed from the failures of its predecessor and proved capable of providing some solutions to the problems that had contributed to the collapse of the tsarist state; these included the pressures engendered during the process of early industrialization and the issues arising out of the agrarian question. The Soviet party-state evolved procedures that served to sustain its organizational strength and enhance its capacity for control over society. Although successful in the early Soviet period, the contribution of these procedures to the maintenance of the system during the period of "developed socialism" is open to some question. Their application to Eastern Europe after World War II has also proved problematic, as the trials and unique solutions produced by the Polish party-state have clearly shown. The "Leninist concept of a socialist revolution had been made to measure for a society held together by a political scaffolding alone, and can offer little guidance for a society with a richer texture" (Bauman 1981). The constitutive role of the party-state has been more constrained in Eastern Europe than it was in Russia; more aware societies in more highly developed territories of Eastern Europe

39

have provided the party-state with less malleable material.
 Still, the meshing together of the Leninist vanguard party with the traditional authoritarian state formed a new structure characterized by some striking strengths. Its particular form of dominance over Russia and associated former tsarist territories, in which these strengths were nurtured and exercised, has proved difficult to comprehend within the categories of political analysis drawn from Western traditions. The notion of a single party commanding a monopoly of power within a political system is already a contradiction in terms, as "a political 'party' can mean only a competing body, competing for a 'part' in 'power'" (Schapiro 1972, 59). Equally, it has been suggested that the influence exerted by the party on the state, both externally and from within through the action of party cells inside the administration, lends a fictional character to that traditional institution of political rule. Insofar as the East European states are used by the party merely to exert its dominance, Lowit (1978) has suggested that the traditional term be abandoned to allow clearer understanding of the political processes at work in that area. Terminological issues aside, it is clear that the system of rule that grew out of the Russian Revolution involved novel characteristics both in its relationship to the society that produced it and in the particular form of political order to which it has given rise. While this order is neither clearly reducible to the more established categories of party or state, the term "party-state" can be used to refer to a new political form that combines elements of both and, more importantly, synthesizes their dual claim to power and sovereignty.
 Party-state dominance over society has been maintained in association with processes assuring party superiority within the overall party-state complex. This occurs in at least two ways: horizontally, in that party organs exercise authority over government and state organizations at the same level (for example, the Politburo dominates the Polish Council of Ministers, while the First Secretary of the party takes precedence over the Prime Minister); and vertically, as a system of strict hierarchical control is exercised within the party according to principles of democratic centralism. By these means central control over the occupancy of positions of authority is maintained, organizational discipline is enforced, and deviations from central policy are prevented. A key role in the process by which central party authority is sustained is played by the practice of <u>nomenklatura</u>. As a highly developed and detailed bureaucratic mechanism, it is one of the more novel and characteristic features of the Communist party-state and one whose role perhaps

warrants further study. Distortions of <u>nomenklatura</u> processes had been evident in Poland well before the collapse of the Gierek regime. Attention was again focused on them in the deliberations of the thirteenth Plenum of the PUWP Central Committee in 1983, when the Jaruzelski administration sought to normalize the political situation.

<u>Nomenklatura</u> in itself is merely a record of institutional posts, "a list of positions, arranged in order of seniority, including a description of the duties of each office" (Harasymiw 1969, 494). Its importance in the system of rule of the party-state and the reason why mention of <u>nomenklatura</u> in the context of Soviet-type societies carries an aura of both status and power is that appointment to such posts requires ratification by an appropriate party committee. This is, of course, particularly true in the case of more important positions and with full-time jobs in the party organization itself. Indeed, precisely because the party <u>nomenklatura</u> extends to all areas and sectors of society, "the party has achieved a deeper and more comprehensive penetration of society than any previous rulers of Russia" (Miller 1982, 21). Thus the <u>nomenklatura</u> procedure is a guarantee of central party control and reflects an important way in which rule is effected through the institutions of the party-state. It is associated with the determination of the central leadership to ensure that the appropriate people be found in all important positions and can therefore be expected to behave in appropriate fashion. After all, cadres can be construed as "deciding everything," in Stalin's well-known phrase.

The importance of this procedure and its apparently characteristic association with the system of rule of the party-state has led to suggestions that it might prove the most reliable guide to the basic social structures and alignments of power within Soviet-type societies. Thus Nove (1975, 615) has seen the Central Committee's nomenclature as a possible "formal definition" of the ruling stratum. Voslensky (1980, 125) has suggested that the 750,000 nomenclature appointees, together with their dependents, constitute the "dominant class in the Soviet Union." <u>Nomenklatura</u> is therefore a fundamental feature of the contemporary party-state and a significant aspect of its system of rule. It may be seen as a mechanism that serves to institutionalize the party-state regime, in that it underpins the dominance of the party-state apparatus over society, counteracting any tendency to the emergence of autonomous social forces and that it acts to integrate the different sectors of the party-state apparatus and to articulate the supremacy of central party organs in the apparatus as a whole.

The dominance of the party-state apparatus is, however, not exerted in a vacuum nor does the nomenklatura process operate in mechanical fashion. The pressures brought to bear by the social movements during the Solidarity period in Poland challenged the supremacy of the party-state and apparently threatened to undermine its base. The movement demanded that the party-state qualify its principle of operation and, although the substance of the social campaign was effectively countered, the points raised during this period have not been without consequence. Frontal attacks were made on the two main ways in which overall party supremacy has been maintained. The detailed control by party bodies of all activities of state and government organizations was criticized; the final agreement dealt with certain associated issues, such as barring party personnel from holding simultaneous office in state bodies. Party and state were thus expected to be decoupled to at least some extent. Similarly, the vertical mechanism assuring central party dominance was subject to qualification with the rebirth of autonomous action in local party cells and the forging of local horizontal links between them, which had formerly been viewed as an unimaginable heresy, according to the dogma of democratic centralism. The nomenklatura procedure was itself questioned and indeed demands for its rectification appeared as point twelve in protocol of the original Gdansk Agreements in response to the demand that "leading and managing cadres are selected by virtue of their qualifications not their party affiliation" (Ascherson 1981, 280).

Thus key features of the party-state came under attack and processes assuring the institutionalization of the party-state regime were disrupted. Central party control over appointments, not just in state and government bodies but also within the party apparatus, was threatened. As the social movement launched by Solidarity gained momentum, democratization gathered pace within the PUWP and greater authority passed to the lower organs of the party. Part of this process involved greater freedom in the election of memebrs of the full-time party staff and more autonomy in the choice of the secretaries heading committees at various levels of the party hierarchy. The democratization movement within the party had been preceded by less institutionalized action and spontaneous criticism of corrupt administrators and party officials. For example, by November 1980 those in Czestochowa, Jelenia Gora, and Bielsko Biala were starting to be removed under local pressure. The time of greatest renewal within the party and among the key provincial (wojewodztwo) party secretaries was, however, in the late spring of 1981 during the local party conferences.

On average and under normal conditions, a replacement rate of nine of the forty-nine provincial first secretaries might have been expected annually. Between the August strikes and the end of 1980, however, twenty-two changes took place, while the number rose to thirty-one in the first six months of 1981 (author's own research). It was clear that these important party appointments were no longer under the strict control reflected in conventional nomenklatura procedures and that the processes by which the party-state had institutionalized its rule were no longer fully effective.

Poland in 1980 and 1981 provided the clearest example of the problems involved in exercising power through the structures of the party-state and showed the most striking attenuation of the processes by which its regime was institutionalized. This was by no means the first occasion on which the shortcomings of the party-state system had become evident, however. The very longevity and success of the system in the Soviet Union provided the conditions for the growth of new social interests that came to threaten the operation of the system and undermine its effectiveness. Faced with increasing economic problems and the declining responsiveness of party-state structures to control by the central leadership, Khrushchev introduced some institutional innovations that involved the reallocation of responsibilities within party-state structures and threatened the security of officials' tenure. The system's predictability had to be proved its overall effectiveness of operation. It seems clear that the officials' resistance to these changes contributed to the creation of a political situation in which Khrushchev could be removed from the leadership by his colleagues. "Stability of cadres," therefore, became a byword of the Brezhnev administration. The problems had been shelved only to reemerge more starkly in the late 1970s and early 1980s with any solution to them being delayed by Brezhnev's lingering physical and political demise. In 1983 Andropov was quick to attempt a limited reform of the conservative structures of the established party-state and to replace some of its more moribund officials. In the fifteen months following Brezhnev's death, thirty-five of the 158 first secretaries of the regional party committees were changed, the most sweeping changes since the time of Khrushchev. Yet, following Andropov's brief period of tenure, the emergence of Chernenko's leadership suggests a return to greater sensitivity to the conservative inclination of Soviet party-state officials. The issues arising from the "declining vitality and responsiveness of the party apparatus" are not likely to go away, however, and to ignore them "is to risk eventually greater dangers for the system--dangers of a kind that developed for the Polish party" (Odom 1983, 19).

The problems faced by the Polish party-state in 1980 were clearly of a more critical nature. The inefficiency of the apparatus in administering the state-controlled economy contributed to an extensive economic crisis. The criticisms launched by Solidarity and the diverse currents of the social movement against the party-state could thus be presented as purely objective necessities in a rapidly deteriorating situation. At the same time the movement was directed against party hegemony and the system of party-state rule. The criticism had strong social roots: the party's base was less firmly established than in any other country of Eastern Europe, while nomenklatura procedures, with their bias in favor of party members, seemed particularly unjust in a society characterized by strong Catholic convictions. The depth of the Polish crisis, therefore, served to combine attacks on the party-state arising from social dissatisfaction with criticism associated with the clear inability of the apparatus to function, in its own terms and in the eyes of those who shared its underlying principles.

The crisis that became evident in Poland in 1980 involved problems in the operation of the party-state similar to those that had long been evident in the Soviet Union. But the conflicts also arose from attempts to smother a society that had autonomous values and strong elements of self-awareness with the imposition of a party-state apparatus that left no space for the existence of such areas of autonomy. The problems arising from the operation of the apparatus itself were, of course, exacerbated by the difficulties involved in accommodating it to Polish society. It is clear that this was never satisfactorily achieved during the early years of the Polish People's Republic. The forms of the orthodox party-state apparatus were in place, but they were never capable of exercising the transformative power inherent in the original Soviet model: "although institutions usually identified with a socialist order were introduced into Poland after World War II, they either did not take root or else were accepted as part of a new reality in the most superficial of ways" (Fiszman 1975). The institutionalization of the party-state regime was thus a persistent problem in Poland. It is doubtful whether its institutionalization was ever adequate to maintain, in Jowitt's phrase, its "organizational integrity" (1983, 275). This is not particularly surprising in view of the nonrevolutionary origins of the Polish regime. Problems of institutionalization, however, were probably enhanced by the high level of the non-Communist combat ethos that prevailed in postwar Polish society, in comparison with such countries as Hungary and East Germany, where such an ethos was undermined practically and morally by their status as defeated Axis combatants (ibid.). The relatively high popularity of Communist forces in Czechoslovakia and the economic advantages enjoyed by its population greatly facilitated the institutionalization of the party-state regime there.

The process encountered obstacles in Poland that contributed to the problems faced by the elite, and thereby sheds some light on the peculiarities of nomenklatura procedures and other aspects of elite behavior. The persistent factionalism of higher party politics in Poland thus reflected the weak integration within the party-state apparatus that resulted from the problems of regime institutionalization (Lewis 1984). During the 1970s the "carousel of cadres" (or "job roundabout") became a notorious aspect of elite self-protection, as well as a source of low performance levels in specific organizational tasks. At the same time, the apparent interchangeability of cadres could be construed as a surrogate form of elite integration and a mechanism preventing the outbreak of excessive intra-elite conflict. The tolerance and even encouragement of corrupt practices in the 1970s performed similar functions. If ideological and other sources of normative integration were lacking, at least members of the elite were able to develop a material interest in the operation of the system. These seem to be part of the "smokescreen of stylistic variations" that Staniszkis refers to, "the 'double bind' mechanism used in the past with regard to strategic social groups--particularly the power apparatus and managerial strata" (1982, 87). Such variations were part of the final phase of the attempt to develop superficial solutions to the problems of institutionalizing the party-state regime in Poland.

During earlier crises, and particularly immediately after them, when a new leadership hopefully proclaimed its intention of putting the situation to rights and setting the system of rule on a new footing, at least some of these problems had been recognized, although attention was largely restricted to the operation of the party apparatus rather than to that of the party-state system as a whole. Thus in 1956 Gomulka complained that "the Party apparatus became inflated and was either bureaucratized under the conditions of the existing system of work or took on other unhealthy forms" (Zinner 1956, 234-35). Following the dispiriting events of the late Gomulka period, one local party official contributed the following to a Central Committee discussion: "For a long time one could sense there was something terribly wrong with the Party.... We got entangled in the mechanism of power which we ourselves created (Bromke and Strong 1973, 217). After Gierek's fall, Kania also recognized that "one of the most important problems for the party is the operation of its executive apparatus," while one of the key members of the leadership group, Barcikowski, stressed later that "the main source both of this crisis and of former crises has been the paralysis of inner-party democracy, of criticism and control from below, the deformation of cadres policy, and the system by which power is articulated" (Zycie Partii, October 1980 and April 1981).

But the ready tendency to lay the blame for successive crises on the conservatism or the self-serving character of the party apparatus was too simplistic. As Bienkowski, the ex-colleague of Gomulka and a longtime critic of the practice of Polish Communism, has pointed out, if the inefficiency of the apparatus was a major cause of the crisis and organizational chaos in Poland, then the responsibility for that fell to the party leadership, which had formed it and directed its work (1982, 23). Equally, as pointed out in documents published in November 1980 by the Torun party organization, if the good intentions of new sets of leaders had been epeatedly undermined by the character and inclinations of the party apparatus, then "Party reform can only meet with success if there is thoroughgoing reconsideration of the role of the Party's intermediate tiers and the way they operate." In effect the restructuring of the party executive should be sufficiently thoroughgoing to create a situation in which the base of the Party controlled the top (Labour Focus on East Europe 1981, No. 4, p. 52). Reform thus understood would signify genuine change in the class composition of the PUWP This was the veiwpoint associated with the horizontal movement in the party, the tendency that sought to direct relations between local party cells and organizations that only then would be in a position to exert genuine control over the party executive and its apparatus. Otherwise, the broader organizational capacity of the superior committee and its apparatus, which monopolized party exchanges and information between party organs in its sphere of activity, would remain in an unassailable position. This conclusion and the attempt to put it into effect, however, represented an explicit departure from the theory and practice of democratic centralism and threatened the further weakening of the institutionalization of the party-state regime. It directly challenged central party control of the staffing and activities of lower party organs, which, though perhaps much less than fully effective, was one of the ways in which diverse structures were held together and their activities coordinated within the overall framework of the party-state apparatus.

The horizontal movement and other democratizing tendencies within the party directly threatened the institutionalization of the regime and the extent of party-state control over society. It has already been mentioned that the turnover of provincial party committee first secretaries grew rapidly after the August strikes. It is difficult to avoid the suspicion that the threatening Moscow letter of June 1981 was alluding to precisely such developments in its references to "interference with the ranks of the PUWP," the need for "defense of its cadres against enemy attacks," and the idea that local party leaders and conference delegates were "being constituted by people chosen at random" (Nowe Drogi 1981, 30-31). From the point of view of orthodox democratic centralism (represented in its classic form by the Soviet leadership), the degree of autonomy accorded to local party bodies in the proposals of the horizontal movement and the control they claimed over the party executive and its apparatus represented less a process of party democratization than a direct attack on the party. The essence of party leadership and principled party action, according to the theory and practice of the party-state, lay in central party control over society, the state, and the mass of the party itself. By trying to relax this control, the horizontal movement was seeking not so much to strengthen the party as to weaken the party-state. In this view party democratization was merely assisting Solidarity and articulating the demands of a social movement which, by its very existence and claim to legitimacy was challenging the monopolistic authority of the party-state. Insofar as the process was affecting the appointment of such people as party secretaries, which it clearly was, and causing a far higher rate of turnover than would otherwise have been the case, it severely disrupted normal nomenklatura procedures.

The movement of Polish society against the party-state, by preventing the orthodox institutionalization of party structures, also threatened the base of the ruling stratum in Poland. For if the Central Committee nomenklatura could be taken as a reasonably accurate guide to the membership of the ruling stratum, provincial party committee secretaries could be seen as forming an exposed flank of that stratum, as they were one of the few categories within the Central Committee nomenklatura serving outside the center. Since in the Polish case we have the details of the precise content of the nomenklatura of different party bodies, we can be quite specific about the nature of this stratum (Aneks 1981). In terms of the Central Committee nomenklatura as a whole, the only noncentral party appointments under its responsibility were the provincial committee first secretaries, provincial secretaries with specific area responsibilities (sekretarze-resortowi, i.e., those with particular responsibility for organization, industry, ideology, etc.), and the directors of the party schools in Bydgoszcz and

Katowice. The number of provincial secretaries was around 245 throughout the whole of Poland (Zycie Partii, September 1981). In terms of appointments decided by the Politburo itself (which may be taken to constitute the political elite of the ruling stratum), provincial committee first secretaries (forty-nine throughout Poland) were the only noncentral party appointments with which the ruling body of the party concerned itself. Indeed, provincial first secretaries and regional military commanders were the only noncentral appointments reserved for the specific responsibility of the Politburo. The reservation of the leading regional party and military posts suggests the importance they shared in the maintenance of the party-state.

During 1980 and particularly 1981 central party control over regional party appointments was considerably weakened. With the redefinition of relations between state and society that took place after the August strikes, party-state procedures became contaminated by social forces and the process by which central party rule was reproduced became obstructed. The party-state regime and its control of leading political appointments, had hitherto been insulated from the direct influence of social forces. This separation was now over. The party democratization movement came to influence both the rate at which provincial party secretarial appointments were made and the kind of people who were appointed. The differences, at least in statistical terms, were not excessively dramatic and their effect should perhaps not be exaggerated. Nevertheless, the consequences of the change in normal appointment procedures were detectable and the differences that emerged in 1980 and 1981 suggested the direction of the change that might take place if central party control of appointments were again weakened in the future.

In the first half of 1981, the thirty-one provincial party committee first secretaries elected (mostly at local conferences held in preparation for the Extraordinary Party Congress of July), were slightly younger than earlier groups and had been party members for a shorter period of time. Their average age was forty-four (as opposed to forty-five years on average for those appointed between 1975 and 1980) and they had been members of the PUWP for twenty-one years (twenty-three on average for 1975-1980 appointees). Perhaps more significant was the fact that they had spent nine years on average serving in the party's political apparatus, in contrast to the ten years of those appointed between 1975 and 1980 and the eleven years of those appointed as a result of the organizational reform of May and June 1975. They also had a shorter period of experience in posts of general polit-

ical responsibility: thus, for provincial committee appointments, an average of eleven years had elapsed since their first apparatus appointments. Those appointed during the 1975 reform had seventeen years of equivalent experience (all data from author's own research).
 These changes do not appear very striking, but more significant differences emerge if further distinctions are drawn. For instance, of those elected in early 1981, 81 percent had joined the party in 1956 or after, and 68 percent had joined no earlier than 1960. Their experience as party members in the Stalin period was therefore quite limited. Of those appointed between 1975 and 1980, only 43 percent joined in 1956 or after. Differences also emerge in the background of those appointed and elected in the different phases of the post-August reform period. Thus, those appointed in 1980, after the fall of Gierek, were older (forty-eight years on average) and had been party members longer (twenty-four years) than those elected during the first half of 1981, and also those appointed under normal circumstances between 1975 and 1980. Indeed, only 36 percent of those appointed in late 1980 had joined the party in 1956 or after, a lower proportion than those appointed between 1975 and 1980, even though the simple passage of time might have favored a higher proportion. In terms of appointments of provincial first secretaries in the post-August period, then, two distinct waves can be identified: the first, consisting of older men (there were no women) with longer than average party experience and the second, rather younger, with definitely less experience. Appointments after the Extraordinary Congress, the bulk of which were made under the State of War and during the subsequent period of quasi-military normalization, were of people considerably older (an average of forty-eight years of age with longer party experience (twenty-five years).
 Other significant characteristics of the post-August appointments, which apply more directly to nomenklatura procedures and the institutionalization of the party-state regime, concern the declining proportion of new first secretaries with earlier experience as provincial committee secretary or as first secretary of a party committee one level down (i.e., town, plant, district committee). Of those appointed in 1975, or between 1975, and 1980, 89 and 86 percent respectively had served in either one of these two positions. That seemed to be a standard prerequisite for appointment as provincial party committee first secretary. Those who did not have such experience had generally served in posts of analagous importance and responsibility (deputy head of a Central Committee departments, head of youth movement, deputy minister). Those appointed

after August 1980 had served less often in such posts; only 77 and 71 percent of appointments in late 1980 and early 1981, respectively, had had experience as provincial secretary or first secretary of another party committee. Three appointments in 1980 had markedly unusual career backgrounds: one was brought out of retirement following a career as an industrial manager and two had spent most of their working lives teaching in the Polytechnics. Similarly in early 1981, three new secretaries had had no previous experience of sociopolitical work and four had had only restricted apparatus experience on local party committees. Thus limited though clear divergences in the nature of first secretary appointments did appear during the reform period and the weakening of central party control is apparent in the material presented here. On the face of it, such changes might appear to be minor; nevertheless, the nature of individual appointments in such important posts as first secretary of a provincial party committee can be highly sensitive. It is significant, for example, that the first secretary of the Radom committee, where the major demonstrations of 1976 broke out, was the only 1975 appointee with no apparatus or extensive sociopolitical experience. In view of the national impact of such developments, it is not surprising that first secretaries are on the nomenklatura of the Politburo and that clear patterns of career progression and political experience can generally be ascertained under normal conditions.

In the political situation that developed following the August strikes, however, central party control over apparatus appointments, as in many other areas, was challenged and effectively reduced. One consequence of this was the appointment or election of provincial first secretaries who were unlikely to have been placed in such posts earlier. Another aspect of the reduction of central control was the considerably higher rate of appointment and election of provincial secretaries as a general category. Of the approximately 245 provincial committee secretaries within the Central Committee nomenklatura, nine were changed in the first half of 1979 and nine more in the second half. Fourteen were changed in the first half of 1980, but, as the new situation took hold, seventy-six were changed in the second half. As many as 184 were changed in the first half of 1981 and a further fifty-nine during the following six months. The high rate of change continued into the State of War period, as inappropriate personnel were removed and the impact of the party reform movement was eradicated. It was not until the first half of 1983 that as few as sixteen appointments were made, a figure close to the number of changes before the August strikes and the acceleration of the rate of turnover.

It may be queried whether the change in career background characteristics of provincial first secretaries was due to the social contamination of the nomenklatura process and the resurgence of grass-roots party autonomy or to a growing shortage of conventionally trained personnel. It is likely that both elements played a part. Some evidence supports the notion that the pool of suitable party cadres was becoming exhausted, such as the fact that the proportion of first secretaries who were appointed with experience as provincial committee secretary or as first secretary of a lower-level committee, continued to decline after Jaruzelski's assumption of the party leadership. Thus, of those appointed from mid-1981 to the end of 1983, only 59 percent had such experience, the lowest proportion of any of the groups studied. It is possible that the party-state leadership's decision to switch to more direct reliance on the military hierachy as an instrument of rule--the decision which initiated the State of War in December 1981--was due as much to a shortage of appropriate personnel serving in the party apparatus as to overt political opposition. General Dziekan, head of the Central Committee cadres department since October 1981, has taken care to refute suggestions that Poland in the 1980s has seen a disproportionate rise in the political role of the military. He has claimed that until the lifting of the State of War only 103 out of 180,000 leading positions had been occupied by military personnel (Polityka 1981). This is surely a gross underestimation of the political significance of the military. It should be noted that such an important area as the Central Committee secretariat was under the jurisdiction of a military figure even before the introduction of martial law.

Although he tendency to appoint those with less apparatus experience continued into the State of War and after, in other respects the post-December 1981 appointments have differed from those made in the reform period. One of the rare empirical studies of Polish political leadership stated that "the widespread notion that local party leaders are outsiders had no support in our studies" (Siemienska 1983, 130). All the party officials studied had served in two or three posts in the same or a neighboring province before appointment to the relevant party position. Nevertheless, strict central party control is not only a widespread notion, but also a major characteristic of the party-state and an aspect of its nomenklatura procedures. There is, of course, no reason why staff of local origins should not be appointed centrally, and this has frequently been done. When the authority of the party-state has been exercised decisively, as during the State of War, however, the tendency has been to replace leaders who have strong local connections with

others less committed to local interests and thus more responsive to the demands of the center. Of the seven provincial party committee first secretaries replaced during the first half of 1982, the decided majority had strong local associations and known commitments. They included the following:
   1. Fiszbach (Gdansk) had been in his post since 1975 and was known for his strong commitment to the democratization movement in the party. He had been part of Kania's reformist Politburo since December 1980.
   2. Zabinski (Katowice) was one of the first post-August appointments, and had spent seven years as provincial first secretary in neighboring Opole.
   3. Gawronski (Kalisz) was also appointed in October 1980, and had had nearly thirty years of experience in party and state organizations in neighboring Poznan.
   4. Jasinski (Legnica), elected in June 1981, had spent the previous ten years as manager of a local colliery.
   5. Kruk (Lublin) had been in his post since 1977. He and Fiszbach were two of the three provincial first secretaries to remain in their posts from the Eighth Congress (February 1980) till the declaration of the State of War.
   6. Skrzypczak (Poznan), elected in June 1981, had been engaged in production and management activities, as well as party work, in the local Cegielski works for over twenty years.
Kociolek (Warsaw), the seventh of the group, was appointed in November 1981 and was clearly different from other members of the group. He had initially been appointed first secretary of the Warsaw town committee, which had an importance equal to that of a provincial committee, in 1964 at the age of thirty-one. He then served as first secretary in the Gdansk committee until shortly before the 1970 demonstrations. He was there during the deployment of the armed forces and doubt still persists over his role in their use. Having served in ambassadorial posts during the 1970s, he was clearly imposed on a reluctant Warsaw in 1980 by an insistent Kania. In that situation he was regarded as "the representative of the party's most conservative forces" (Korybutowicz 1983, 48). This action made it clear that the Warsaw party base was being secured by a dependable apparatchik in order to forestall any repetition of the part played by the Warsaw organization in 1956. In 1982 Kociolek was removed and transferred as ambassador to Moscow.
   Several of these secretaries headed committees in major industrial centers that had been bases of working-class opposition to the military regime. Turnover in the secretarial group of these provincial com-

mittees had also been generally high: thus in Katowice, apart from the first secretary, five other secretaries were replaced; four were changed in Gdansk and three removed in Warsaw. Legnica, Lublin, Poznan and Torun also had above average rates of secretarial change. In some cases it was clear that the replacement of the first secretary was directly linked with the threat of opposition to the regime. Thus Skrzypczak was replaced by an air force political officer to prevent demonstrations from taking place to mark the anniversary of the 1956 Poznan revolt (The Times 1983, June 25). The other new appointments also had fewer direct links with the locality and the provincial party committee. Thus the new appointment in Gdansk (Bejger) had a long association with the shipping industry and trade but had spent the previous five years in Helsinki. Wilk (Legnica) came straight from four years spent in the Central Committee organization, his earlier party apparatus experience had been some 200 kilometers from Legnica. Wozniak (Warsaw) had been a Politburo member from February 1982 and had occupied various central posts, although none in the Warsaw party organization. It is notable that in cases in which the new first secretaries did have strong local associations, they were not with the party organization or even with more general sociopolitical posts within the party-state apparatus. Messner (Katowice) and Skrzydlo (Lublin) had both developed their careers exclusively within academic institutions, while Janicki (Kalisz) had spent the preceding twenty years in local industrial production and management. Thus none of the three had experience in any local party apparatus as full-time employees.

It seems clear then that the disruption of the nomenklatura procedure occasioned by the social movement has continued into the period of militarized normalization and that the institutionalization of the party-state regime in Poland remains correspondingly uncertain. It is significant, for example, that public disagreement over the nature and political character of the party political apparatus resurfaced in the second half of 1983 and that some decidedly defensive articles appeared in the organizational periodical of the party (Zycie Partii 1983, September 28).

The effects of the social movement of 1980-1981 and the associated party reform movement are still felt. Those "elected" to party committee secretaryships may formally serve for only two terms. Appointees to the party apparatus (e.g., those holding such posts as instructor and inspector) have therefore lost the view of a clear pattern of career advancement and professional security (ibid.). Frustration and conflict arising form such blockages have previously proved to be of considerable political significance in other contexts. Yet for the Polish leadership simply to abandon these provisions would also be unacceptable, as this would imply a reversion to the thoroughly discredited practices of the pre-Solidarity period. The nature and operation of the nomenklatura system itself remains a live issue. Central party control over appointments clearly grew in the later Gierek years and came to have increasingly detrimental effects on the operation of the Polish economy and political system. There are signs that military figures are eager to restrict the degree of formal party control, a move which does not seem to be wholly acceptable to the Central Committee (Polityka 1983, November 13). So the emergence of the Polish military into the political limelight has not served to eliminate the problems in the operation of the party-state apparatus. Many of the weaknesses in the institutionalization of the regime in Poland remain. The full consequences of the movement that erupted in Polish society in 1980 are yet to be experienced.

REFERENCES

Aneks 1981 (25).
Ascherson, Neal. 1981. The Polish August: the self-limiting revolution. New York: Penguin.
Bauman, Zygmunt. 1981. "On the maturation of Socialism." Telos 47 (Spring).
Bienkowski, Wladyslaw. 1982. Rachunek partyjnego sumienia. Chicago: Polonia Books.
Bromke, Adam and J. Strong, eds. 1973. Gierek's Poland. New York.
Fiszman, Joseph R. 1975. "Poland: The pursuit of legitimacy." I. Volgyes, ed. Political Socialization in Eastern Europe. New York.
Harasymiw, Bogdan. 1969. "Nomenklatura: The Soviet Communist Party's leadership recruitment system." Canadian Journal of Political Science 2.
Jowitt, Kenneth. 1983. "Soviet neo-traditionalism: the political corruption of a Leninist regime." Soviet Studies 35.
Korybutowicz, Z. 1983. Grudzien 1970. Paris: Kultura.
Labour Focus in Eastern Europe 1981, No. 4.
Lewis, Paul G. 1984. "Institutionalization and political change in Poland." Neil Harding, ed. The State in Socialist Society. Albany, N.Y.: SUNY Press.
Lowit, Thomas. 1979. "Y-a-t-il des etats en Europe de l'Est." Revue Francaise de Sociologie 20.
Miller, Jacob. 1982. "The Communist Party: trends and problems." Archie Brown and Michael Kaser, eds. Soviet Policy for the 1980s. London.
Nove, Alec. 1975. "Is there a ruling class in the USSR?" Soviet Studies, 22.
_____ 1983. "The class nature of the Soviet Union revisited." Soviet Studies, 35.
Nowe Drogi July 1981.
Odom, W. 1983. "Choice and Change in Soviet Politics." Problems of Communism, 32.
Polityka November 19, 1983.
Schapiro, Leonard B. 1972. Totalitarianism. New York: Praeger.
Siemienska, Renata. 1983. "Local Party Leaders in Poland." International Political Science Review 4.
Staniszkis, Jadwiga. 1982. "Martial law in Poland." Telos 54.
Voslensky, Mikhail. 1980. La Nomenklatura: les privilegies in URSS. Paris.
Zinner, Paul E., ed. 1956. National and popular revolt communism in Eastern Europe. New York: Columbia University Press.
Zycie Partii, October 1980, April 1981, September, December 1983.

4
Constitution and Functioning of a Civil Society in Poland

Maria Markus

This paper focuses on the transformations of Polish society following the events of 1980-1981. Some of these transformations will, we hope, resist attempts at normalization and survive to give meaning to those two years as more than the newest tragic but heroic pages in the history of Poland. I shall confine myself to identifying these effects as the constituents of the new civil society in Poland. Such a formulation demands a few preliminary definitions.

What is meant by civil society? It is certainly not an unambiguous concept with a clearly defined meaning. The concept has not only changed over time, but is also currently applied in various social systems to designate divergent social phenomena. One might justifiably ask whether the term itself has a constant meaning or whether the social sphere seen as belonging to civil society at least has some consistent functions.

The concept of civil society is used here in its modern meaning, as opposed to the traditional concept of societas civilis, by which philosophers from Cicero to Kant essentially designated a politically articulated society within the institutional framework of a state. Certainly, civil society in its modern sense does not mean society without a state. The political organization of the state and the basic assumptions underlying it are, in a sense, preconditions of a more-or-less autonomous civil society. One cannot identify civil society with the private sphere, in opposition to the state-organized public one. It is the public sphere, the structure of self-organization of society outside, though still connected with, the institutional framework of the state. The most important features of civil society, whatever other historically concrete characteristics it may display, are formal equality of civil and social rights, conscious acceptance of (or at least tolerance for) the plurality of interests, and publicity, in the sense of openness, and lack of secrecy in its functioning.

One may identify the major function of civil society as linking the goals of the state's activity with those of the structurated population through different concrete mechanisms of mediation. This function involves: (1) the elaboration of those normative social structures through which group identities and the encompassing collective identity of a given society are defined, including the definition of its traditions, its hierarchy of values, and its norms of social behavior; (2) control over state policies from the viewpoint of their consistency with the socially constitutive systems of values; and (3) societal self-defense when such consistency is violated. These functions may be treated as generally fulfilled by all historical forms of civil society, though the concrete mechanisms through which these functions were performed have varied.

Civil society was constituted in its classical form in the West during the seventeenth and eighteenth centuries. It was above all a basically homogeneous sphere encompassing mainly the ascending bourgeoisie acting as a "universal class." Despite being firmly embedded in the institution of private property, it was able to formulate without great difficulty the demands of equality of individual rights and general accessibility of the public sphere. When the extension of the franchise, education, the press, and other means of mass communication resulted in the expansion of this public body, it lost its homogeneity and became an area of competitive interests and often violent conflicts which could only be resolved or mitigated through increased institutional interference by the state.

The civil society of contemporary mass democracies in the West has been organized according to a principle of competition among a large number of formal organizations. These organizations act as pressure, groups, potentially in opposition to each other, but ideally reaching some form of social consensus. The consensus is facilitated by the fact that members of society participate in several such organizations; in addition, there are effective mechanisms of hegemony ensuring a significant degree of artificial homogenization of the public. As a result, there has been a historical trend toward weakening the critical function of the public sphere.

As pointed out by several authors, the most recent tendencies of the reconstruction and restructuration of civil society in the West address a different set of problems from those created by the attempt at the constitution of civil society in Poland. The differences are defined mainly by the fact that, despite the increasing role and interference of the state in the West, the formal and legal structure of the state itself was originally shaped by principles formulated within the civil society itself. Therefore, possible conflicts between the state and society are in a sense pacified by this institutionalized legal structure of confrontation and compromise.

All this indicates that social movement toward the establishment of an independent public sphere, of which the events of 1980-1981 in Poland represented only the latest stage, had no real model to follow. It had to innovate both theoretically and practically, but it also had to readjust its strategies and aims constantly in accordance with changing internal and external circumstances and pressures.

Since the mid-1970s the majority of groups within the Polish democratic opposition have pointed to the absence of civil society as one of the most problematic features of the post-Stalinist regime in Poland. Civil society was understood not as a conglomerate of egotistic individuals and competing formal organizations, but as the self-organization of all segments of society, generating collective support for initiatives concerning the representation of interests and the defense of civil rights. It was envisaged as a mediating structure between the closest circles of family and friends on the one hand and the state on the other. This conception was already outlined by Kolakowski (1971). Similar ideas can also be found in the DiP report, which criticized the absence of civil society in Poland as the main factor in social schizophrenia (Vale 1981).

The program of action has thus concentrated on the democratic self-organization of social solidarity and cooperation outside the institutional framework of the state. Several organizations (NOWA-publishers, the Flying University, KOR, Student's Solidarity Groups, The Movement for Defense of Human and Civil Rights, Solidarity, and Rural Solidarity) were the result of this conscious attempt at the constitution of a civil society, serving as "structures of social solidarity and participation, bypassing state power altogether or relating to it only on the level of negotiation and compromise" (Arato 1981, 24-29). In the process of the emergence of civil society in Poland, one can distinguish three basic aspects that simultaneously constitute the main focus of its internal disputes and conflicts. These three closely interconnected but analytically separable aspects were: (1) the principles of organization of the new public sphere; (2) the main areas of its concern and activities; and (3) the forms and means of the institutionalization of the relationship between the state and civil society.

Because the Polish movement accepted political realities (for example the supremacy of the Communist Party), the organizational principles of civil society became one of the most important issues. The main principles of organization were solidarity, plurality, undistorted communication, and participation. The institutional structure organized by the party-state apparatus was recognized as oppressive to the whole society and inimical to an identity of interests among various social groups. It was also acknowledged that social diversity could easily generate conflict, so that a constant need existed for a ranking of demands and for compromise between competing interests; this could only be achieved through mutual social solidarity. It was further assumed that such a compromise should and could be reached only if various social groups organized themselves, formulated their needs, and negotiated some degree of consensus among themselves. Solidarity was thus envisaged and exercised not as an imposed formula but as a voluntary act of mutual understanding. The organization of the movement that took Solidarity as its name constantly supported the legalization of other organizations representing divergent structures of interest. This attitude produced several impressive examples of mutual solidarity, such as support for the legalization of farmers' and students' organizations and participation by white-collar Solidarity members in actions for free Saturdays though most of them did not benefit from the achieved agreements (Bialecki 1982).

Among the significant factors that made possible such a suspension of important social tensions between and within various groups and strata and that facilitated their mutual practical understanding, following two were most influential. First, civil society in Poland was constituted not only around the structures of economic interests, but also around shared moral and cultural values. The concept of "moral renewal" was included in Solidarity's program. This provided a basis for agreement and cooperation between different groups. Other common goals included the establishment of an independent structure of information, an autonomous system of social education, and other projects. Second, the state's monopoly of control over the economy in Poland, and in Eastern Europe in general, has meant that primary stratification is created within the institutional framework of the state. Thus common action can take place, even in cases of conflicting interests, providing they are articulated as demands directed toward and against the state. Under the specific conditions of Poland, the conflicts of interests that occur among all elements of social structure have been directed or channeled against the "main center of power," which is held responsible for producing them (Galeski 1982). The sharp conflict between farmers and the urban population over the relative price of agricultural products can thus be rationalized as an effect of political-administrative decisions. Prices are administratively formulated without reference to production costs, economic factors, or a sense of social justice. The primary conflict can be superseded because it is seen as the consequence of a purely political manipulation of the distribution of privilege, producing insecurity and dependence for both privileged and underprivileged.

The first of these homogenizing factors formed the basis of social solidarity through the active participation of members of the public in the creation of informal social networks and in society's attempt at emancipation; the second acted in a rather negative way, by identifying the common enemy as the source of deprivation to all layers of society, stipulating therefore forms of unity "against" rather than "for."

The principle of solidaristic pluralism, despite its merits, faced a number of difficulties that produced several inconsistencies. Despite the mass character of Solidarity, there existed an objective asymmetry among its participants. As a result of its relatively early legalization, combined with the absence of legal rules for the organization of other autonomous groups, Solidarity obtained the position and prestige of the first among equals. The necessity to integrate existing movements and to counter state power with unified demands naturally strengthened the integrative function of the union. The coincidence of these factors contributed to the inconsistency of the movement's limited formula as a "pure" trade union. Subsequently, it produced unresolved internal tensions, which increased as the situation became more complex. The fact that the movement followed the principle of pluralism prevented the internal differences from being clearly articulated, discussed, and either resolved or smoothed out by negotiations (Staniszkis 1982). Unity often appeared in opposition to the actions of the authorities; it neither resolved nor effectively silenced the existing internal splits and conflicts.

Still other obstacles on the way to pluralism derived from the absence of institutionalized, legally sanctioned forms of negotiation between the state and the self-organized civil society. This situation often created an opportunity for the state to decide whom to consider as the representative of the society and with whom to negotiate. Apart from other negative effects, such a situation led to the violation of both the democratic principle of organization of civil society and its principle of non secrecy and openness in decision making. In this way, internal conflicts were externally created.

The question of the main terrain of social activity centered around the important issue of participation versus nonparticipation in the existing power structures. Declarations concerning the nonpolitical character of Solidarity were at least partly dictated by strategic or tactical reasons, but the refusal either to participate in or replace state power was consistently built into the general conception of social self-organization and self-defense, accepting plurality as a fundamental societal characteristic and value. The desire to build and maintain the duality of the state and civil society, whatever the tactical or strategic conceptions involved, was one of the most important theoretical and practical issues formulated by the recent movement in Poland. The commitment to such a duality was clearly formulated by Solidarity's leaders and advisers. In their opinion, a social movement should not attempt to become a party, since once the party gains state power, society loses its organization and defense. The question of where the dividing line between participation and non-participation in power should be, however, remained unresolved. The issues generating the strongest controversies, conflicts, and an even greater number of inconsistencies in the movement's own strategy were: first, whether democratic participation in the newly emerging civil society meant involvement in the informal social networks it was supposed to create; second, whether participation should be extended to include different forms of self-governing or controlling bodies within the state-organized sphere of the economy (and some other areas); and third whether civil society should undertake the responsibilty for the working of society or only formulate its needs and demands. It is clear that even if the idea of a political take-over (understood as the abolition of the existing state structure) was more or less consistently rejected throughout the whole period by the main core of the movement, attitudes toward participation in political power not only changed gradually, but also created the main dividing line between various factions within this movement from the beginning.

The range of formulated alternatives was wide and extended from those of an essential reconstitution of the monolithic party-controlled system to proposals of a liberal democratic type of social arrangement. Four alternative models for the organization of civil society and its relationship with the state were formulated during this period. The basic differences concerned the level of politicization of civil society and the combination of pluralism with different forms of corporatism. According to Arato (1981), none of these models challenged the very existence of the party-state although they seriously limited its functions.

The state-corporatist model of civil society was favored at some stage by the reformist elements in the party. It consisted of a camouflaged attempt to co-opt autonomous social organizations. This model (sponsored by PAX) was later revitalized as the Front of National

Understanding, which was supposed to consist of representatives of some basic social organizations and institutions. The idea of reconciliation was, to a limited degree, supported by the union in late 1981, since it was seen as an emergency, extemporaneous measure. Official negotiations which involved the government, the church, and Solidarity, failed for several reasons. The negotiations started in late fall, 1981, when the conflict between the social movement and the state was too advanced to be controlled. Aware of this situation, state officials tried to conceal their preparation for martial law and did not treat the negotiations seriously. If the idea of "understanding" was to succeed, the Front had to take the form of a coalition between equal partners that represented actual social forces. The government, however, wanted to use reconciliation" as a form of state corporatism, by including as nominal partners a number of socially insignificant but party-controlled organizations (old trade unions, Peasant Party, Democratic Party, and others).

An alternative model of civil society was that of social corporatism. It consisted of pluralistic structures organized into a cooperative network and opposed to the monolithic system of the state. This option assumed communication between the two structures in the form of constant negotiations under the control of public opinion. Although various concepts of such a model have been proposed, none resolved the problem of concrete forms of arbitration that would guarantee fair compromises.

Finally, there were two polarized ideas concerning civil society. The first suggested the total depoliticization of the civil society and the concentration of its activities around the reorganization of basic social structures. The second aimed at the total repoliticization of Polish civil society and envisaged either the redefinition of Solidarity as a political party or the organization of a labor party, based on the existing structures of Solidarity, but without abolishing these structures. Neither of these ideas articulated the relationship between new principles and forms of social organizations and the old structures of the party-state.

For the democratic opposition this new projected realm of relationships between the state and civil society seemed to be feasible under the form of a "new" social contract. The moderate elements in the party leadership at times seemed to agree with such an idea, but the predominant core of the party apparatus and its leadership regarded any attempt at the establishment of a dual structure as an intolerable provocation that could only be answered at the opportune moment by force. Whether this last outcome could have been avoided is difficult to say. The opinion that it was avoidable, had Solidarity restricted itself to a role similar to that of Western trade unions, does not really clarify this point since such a compromise was impossible. The social conditions of the establishment of Solidarity were totally different from those under which Western unions were organized. Therefore, aside from the fact that the trade-unionist formula was too narrow from the very beginning, Solidarity as a trade union had several functions because it was confronted by the state as the main and near monopolistic employer. It is also clear that, under the legal, political, and cultural conditions of state socialism, such a restriction would mean the co-optation, integration, and assimilation of Solidarity that is, its truncation as a movement.

What then are the possible lasting effects of the tragically suppressed Polish movement that aimed to create and to legalize a new civil society? First of all, while Solidarity suffered a defeat, it was not destroyed. The formal network of the democratic mass organization has disappeared, but the informal one, both in its legal and illegal forms, remains. It continues its activities in the fields of communication, culture, and information, even if its scope is drastically reduced. Publishing activity has been resumed. A sense of the collective dignity of the population constitutes the lasting achievement of the movement, even if its organizational core has been shattered. Research on the impact of the events of 1980-1981 indicates that a new image of the worker has emerged as that of a man socially committed, conscious of his own power and solidarity, capable of unselfishness and sacrifices (Bialecki 1982, 118). Although the longevity of this change is questionable under the pressures of everyday life, "the promotion of solemn values as formulated in the slogans of the 'movement of moral renewal' will leave some permanent traces in social memory" (ibid.). One can assume that these effects will survive not only as elements in the historical recollection of the people (in a purely symbolic manner), but also in the social psychology as factors influencing future actions as well.

The Solidarity movement influenced another chain of events, which should not be underestimated. These are the effects upon the formal institutional structures of both the party and the state. It is usual to say that the Polish events left these structures untouched or paralyzed. This is only a half truth. The identity crisis within the apparatuses of the state and the party and within the party membership in general caused some formal changes to occur. Even a purely verbal adherence to Marxist ideology involves the indispensability of certain theses, among which the historical role of the proletariat and its representation by the party are crucial (Markus 1982). The mass character of Solidarity and the involvement--even the leading role--of the proletariat in it has created an identity crisis which has led to certain structural modifications. It is also obvious that any stabilization of the post-martial law regime would require some modification in the structure and status of the "official" trade unions.

It is difficult to predict what concrete forms these changes will take. It is clear that even if a merely limited normalization is to occur, it has to respond somehow to the lasting effects created by the short-lived existence of a civil society in Poland. Therefore, it seems that the often-posed alternative between the Czech or the Hungarian model of normalization is a false one. In the past it was impossible to go beyond the basic Soviet model, but the post-Stalinist period has brought about a diversification of this model, creating hybrids. Although the Hungarian model is the most attractive to both sides, it is hardly a solution to the problems posed by the Polish movement. It has neither created a new relationship between the political and the economic spheres nor introduced any kind of built-in mechanisms for social control or influence from below. Any kind of genuine social participation is as nonexistent in this submodel as it is in any other variant of the Soviet model. The totally paternalistic structure of the usurping representation is maintained untouched, only functioning in a much more orderly and enlightened way in comparison with the majority of other East European societies. The liberalization of the regime has meant basically the neutralization of the population through the depoliticization of everyday life and through the generation of a complex system of achievable but not safeguarded concessions and liberties. Polish history has yet to create its own compromise based on its own potential and expressing its own relation of social forces. If it were not so dangerous and senseless for a social scientist to play the role of prophet, one could say that it will probably be a compromise much less economically comfortable but more politically flexible than its Hungarian counterpart.

Has the Solidarity movement in Poland created any model for the self-organization of a nonbourgeois civil society? Even if not a model, the Polish movement did anticipate and demonstrate a number of the characteristics that a civil society of a new type should possess. The Polish events also demonstrated that such a civil society cannot be stabilized without basic changes in the structure of the political state. The Polish movement of emancipation was, from its very inception, faced with just this paradox.

REFERENCES

Arato, Andrew. 1981. "Civil Society versus the State: Poland 1980-81," Telos 47 (Spring).
Bialecki, Ireneusz. 1982. "Solidarity: The Roots of the Movement." Sisyphus 3. Warsaw: Polish Scientific Publishers.
Galeski, Boguslaw. 1982. "Social Structure: Conflict of Interests." Sisyphus 3. Warsaw: Polish Scientific Publishers.
Kolakowski, Leszek. 1971. Tezy o nadziei i beznadziejnosci. Paris: Societe Internationale d'Editions.
Markus, Maria. 1982. "Overt and Covert Modes of Legitimation." T. H. Rigby and F. Feher, eds. Political Legitimation in Communist States. New York: Macmillan.
Staniszkis, Jadwiga. 1982. "Self-Limiting Revolution." Sisyphus 3. Warsaw: Polish Scientific Publishers.
Vale, Michael, ed. 1981. Poland: The State of the Republic. London: Pluto Press.

5
The Catholic Church in Defense of Civil Society in Poland
Bogdan Szajkowski

In Search of the Concept of Civil Society

The concept of civil society is an ambiguous one. Despite several recent attempts to find an adequate formulation, the concept remains as problematic as ever (see Urry 1981; Althuser 1969; Poulantzas 1978; Jakubowski 1976; Miliband 1969.) In order to indicate the common features and functions of civil societies in different social systems, it seems appropriate to indicate the main stages in the evolution of the concept.

In his *Philosophy of Right*, Hegel defined civil society as a sphere lying between the family and the state (1965, 123-24). The purpose of such a society was utility; its social basis and historically active element was the third estate. It was seen as an economic system that contained within itself guarantees for rational behavior and progress, needing to delegate only limited powers to the political system. In such a concept of society, economic interests were deemed to have a strong claim to support political authority as the leading goal-determining subsystem of society. The concept thus involved not only the sphere of economic relations and the formation of classes, but also the administration of justice and the organization of the police force, which are the two facets of traditional public law. In other words, for Hegel civil society was the sphere of economic relations together with their external regulations according to the principles of the liberal state.

Marx rearranged Hegel's hierarchical order, in which the existence of family and civil society had flowed from the prior existence of the state, and emphasized that political institutions were posterior

---

The author would like to record his gratitude to the British Academy for providing a grant that made possible the discussion of ideas contained in this paper.

67

to social conditions. "Hegel," he wrote, "starts from the State and makes man into the subjective aspect of the State" whereas, in fact, "just as religion does not make man, but man makes religion, so the constitution does not make the people, but the people make the constitution" (Marx 1973, vol. 2,p.65). For Marx, the civil society comprised the entire material interaction among individuals at a particular evolutionary stage of the productive forces. In The German Ideology, which contains one of Marx's most important extracts on the subject, he wrote:

> The form of intercourse determined by the existing productive forces at all previous historical stages, and in its turn determining these, is civil society.... Already here we see how this civil society is the true source and theatre of all history held hitherto, which neglects the real relationships and confines itself to high-sounding dramas of princes and states.... Civil Society... embraces the whole commercial and industrial life of a given stage and, in so far transcends the State and the nation, though, on the other hand again, it must assert itself in its foreign relations as nationality and inwardly must organise itself as State.
> (Marx 1973, vol. 1, pp. 38-76)

This formulation was later reinforced by Engels in his essay on Feuerbach with simple and striking clarity. "The State and the political order is the subordinate, and civil society, the realm of economic relations - the decisive element (Engels 1973, vol. 3, p. 369) In other words, it is not the state that conditions and regulates civil society, but civil society that conditions and regulates the state. Jean L. Cohen, however, has pointed out in her recent book, Class and Civil Society: The Limits of Marxian Critical Theory (1983), that Marx appears to have formulated not one but three variants of the relations between the state and civil society.

In his early writings he increasingly viewed the separation of state and civil society as itself the cause of political and social alienation. He tended to identify civil society straightforwardly with the bellum omnia contra omnes of market society. From this point onward, democracy was associated in his works not with the expansion but with the suppression of civil society. By the time of the Manifesto his hostility to civil society had become more pronounced and the milieu reduced to being the surface expression of a deeper reality. According to Cohen, his break with historical materialism in the "mature" writings and his return from the dialectics of history to the dialectics of capitalism also meant recognition (in the Grundise at

least) that the historical preconditions for the development of capitalism were as much political as economic.
It should be borne in mind that for Marx the institutions of civil society were inextricably linked with his account of class, which displays a radical hostility to it. Consequently, these assumptions were bound to narrow quite considerably the range of enquiry as to the conceptual framework of civil society, its structures and its institutions, as well as its theoretical impact on other post-Marxian societies.
Gramsci, who departed not only from Hegelian usage but also from Marx's equation of civil society with the material substructure, identified civil society with the ideological superstructure, the institutions and technical instruments that create and diffuse models of thought. In one of the most important texts in the Prison Notebooks, he distinguished between political society (dictatorship, coercive apparatus, or entity for the purpose of assimilating the popular masses to the type of production and economy of a given period) and civil society (hegemony of a social group over the entire national society exercised through so-called private organizations, such as the church, the trade unions, the schools, and others) (Gramsci 1971, 12).
Although Gramsci's perspective is highly illuminating in the context of this paper, it does not, however, provide a satisfactory theoretical framework within which one can understand the structures, institutions, and plurality, to use Cohen's term, of contemporary "emancipatory struggles" (Cohen 1983). These emancipatory struggles have common components or institutions in both the West and the East, such as feminism, ecological concerns and pacifism to name just a few. Yet the Marxist tradition has shown little ability to comprehend the diversity of contemporary struggles for liberation that are not based on class.
This tendency perhaps might explain why so little attention has been given to the concept of civil society and to its role in the new social and economic conditions of "real existing socialism." As Arato has rightly pointed out, those writers on the Soviet Union and Eastern Europe who employ the concept in their analysis have used the term without adequate explanation and justification (Arato 1981).
In an illuminating way Misztal has pointed out that such an approach is due mainly to the Marxian tradition itself, which sees the state as secondary to the economy (see chapter 1 of this volume). Such an approach effectively rules out any serious consideration of the emergence and role of civil society vis-a-vis the state in socialist countries. According to Misztal, society produces two forms of social reality. One is the state, historically an earlier formu-

lation, which is meant to be the organizational skeleton of society designed to ensure its well-being. Due to the process of the atomization of the state, society loses its control over it and eventually becomes dominated by its own product.

The second form of social reality that exists as a societal product is social movement. It is meant to promote social change and to defend society against the controlling and coercive functions of the state. In effect, society becomes caught between two inherently opposed forms of reality--the state and social movement. This multiple involvement causes society to transform itself; the transformation process leads to the emergence of civil society. Therefore, civil society is a derivative of society's two products and cannot be abstracted from it (see chapter 10 of this volume).

Dissent, which is by definition excluded from the state's encouraged behavior, seeks to become an element in social movement and to gain control over it. The closer the link between social movement and civil society, the more direct the impact of dissent on the latter.

Misztal's ideas provide useful suggestions for further investigation into much neglected areas of societal relations under "existing socialism" and in particular into the relationship between social movement and civil society, as well as the latter's relation to dissent. For the concept of civil society, see chapter 4 of this volume.

The Church and the State in Historical Perspective*

The Roman Catholic Church in Poland has been a national institution for centuries. Embedded in the national fabric, Polish Catholicism represents not only a system of religious beliefs and sacramental acts, but also the embodiment of Polish cultural values and traditions. The long historical association of Polish Catholicism and Polish ethnicity, as well as their reciprocal influence, has resulted in an almost inseparable integration of the church and nationalism. For centuries the church has exerted a considerable influence on popular attitudes toward political ideologies and institutions. Poland's national identity has recently found its modern form through, and in conflict with, the state, which had been continuously weakened since the end of the seventeenth cen-

---

*In various points in this paper I shall draw on material in my recently published book, Next to God... Poland: Politics and Religion in Contemporary Poland. London: Frances Pinter (Publishers), 1983; New York: St. Martin's Press, 1983.

tury. Conflicts between the church and the state developed into a mechanism that identified Catholicism with national identity; consequently the overwhelming majority of Poles perceive any threat to Catholicism as a threat to the existence of their national identity. In defense of the latter they therefore tend to congregate around the church and religious values.

In more recent times the state has thus been continuously faced with a rival authority whose national role stretches back to the Middle Ages and whose roots in society are very deep. The cultural pattern of Polish national ideology has religious and patriotic components and is closely tied to ideas of democracy. It still informs the national and political consciousness and consequently affects both the consciousness of contemporary Poles and the ideology of the church, which has to take into account the beliefs and aspirations of those who are its social base.

Since the end of World War II, attempts to legitimize the Communist regime in Poland have encountered several obstacles, two of which appear to be particularly relevant here. The first was that Communism came from the East and was brought by the Russians, a people whose state had been in competition with Poland since the sixteenth century. The second obstacle in Poland was the fact that Communism was installed in Poland in 1944 by the Soviet Union, which is at least formally guided by Marxism-Leninism, an outlook whose principles are fundamentally at odds with those of Catholicism.

The Catholic Church in Poland has always been the strongest church in Eastern Europe. After its victory during the Counter-Reformation in the seventeenth century, it ruled unchallenged over the souls of the Polish people. The church enjoyed exceptional influence and wealth, accommodating itself to changing political currents and circumstances. The move of the Polish borders some 500 kilometers to the west meant that for the first time in Polish history, and uniquely in Eastern Europe, the Polish nation was religiously and ethnically homogeneous. The church represented great power, uniting some 90 percent of the population within its organization and behind its ideology.

When the country fell under Communist rule, a new era of direct encounters between the Catholic Church and Communism began. The church had a coherent, uniform organization, more efficient and certainly not inferior to that of the ruling Communist party. More importantly, however, the church had a broader basis of social support than the Communists. The peasants, who then formed the majority of the population and who had originally benefited from the agrarian reform carried out by the new regime almost immediately after its formation, soon became aware of the real agricultural policies of the regime. As they opposed the forcible collectivization of their newly acquired land, they became the target of abuse, persecution, and victimization. They have remained the strongest and most faithful ally of the church. The workers, many of whom were of peasant stock and in whose name the Communists claimed to have seized and wielded power, were soon disillusioned as well, because of the ineffective economic policies of the government. Most of the intelligentsia, who largely consisted of members of the former landed gentry and who after the war absorbed the remnants of that class, were naturally opposed to the Communist regime. Even for those who were by no means religious, the church offered the only opportunity of openly expressing disapproval of the government—by attending Sunday Mass. The church pulpit became a unique source of the uncensored word, a voice eminently concerned with the material and nonmaterial well-being of the people of Poland.

The church in Poland, despite the contradictions of its own objectives in relation to those of the power elite, acquired the state's recognition because of its high social position and the influence it had over society. Many Poles, perhaps the majority, looked to the church, in the absence of other legitimate mechanisms of politicization, not only for spiritual guidance but also for political direction. The church had resisted attempts to be drawn into a framework of political opposition and to be reduced to a supporting role in the new Communist power elite and the system. In order to achieve its ideological goals, it has elaborated a complex strategy of selective involvement, engagement, and criticism. For example, it supported the distribution of land under the land reform of 1944, which expropriated all large estates including those of the church itself, but objected to the collectivization of agriculture. It stipulated that such a policy was only to open the channels of social, cultural, and political involvement for the working class and farmers, but castigated the regime for blocking the promotion to higher positions of professed members of the Catholic intelligentsia. It backed the reconstruction of the country, but deplored restrictions on the construction of churches. It supported the nationalization of industry but strongly criticized the development of statism. Over the years of uneasy coexistence between state and church since 1945, there have been periods of sharp dramatic struggle followed by spells of tranquility and compromise. On the whole, the church has held its ground in the defense of both its own spiritual mission and its place within Polish society. Indeed the moral authority of the church has grown even greater and has been recognized not only by the faithful but by nonbelievers as well.

The turning point in church-state relations came in 1956, in the aftermath of the workers' riots in Poznan, the reemergence of Wladysaw Gomulka as the leader of the ruling PUWP, and the release from house arrest of the Roman Catholic Primate Stefan Wyszynski. In this explosive internal and international situation, with Russian tanks rolling across Poland, the new leadership of the party turned to the church for support. Wyszynski assumed the role of mediator between the power elite and the rebellious working class. In a sermon indicative of his, and the church's, approach to national emergencies, he stated:

> Poles know how to die magnificently ... But, beloved Poles also need to know how to work magnificently. A man dies but once, and is quickly covered in glory. But through work he gives long years in trouble, hardship, pain and suffering. This is a greater heroism.
> (Szajkowski 1983, 17)

This quote summarizes adequately not only the Catholic work ethic but also the church's determination to do nothing that might undermine the state and threaten the nation's independence.

The context of the church's role in Poland has been determined not only by the political situation but also to a considerable extent by a hidden sociocultural pluralism that runs counter to socialism as it really exists. The state aims at the subordination of all forms and manifestations of societal life to a center of disposition that serves its ideology. Under this form of socialism all groups and institutions lose their autonomy and subordinate their activities to the objectives of the socialist state. Thus they become at best mandated bodies executing goals ordered from above. The results of this process are the slow disappearance of autonomous social structures and weakly organized social interaction at the grass-roots level. Right after the formation of the Communist regime in Poland, in an effort to forestall that kind of process, the church broadened its activities beyond strictly religious matters and performed several important socio-pastoral functions. Among the most significant appear to have been its tutelary (i.e. educational and community activities), integrative, and critical functions; this role has been possible because of the absence of formal pluralistic structures in the country. In addition, these activities have been and continue to be an important factor in neutralizing the regime's efforts in the secularization (atheization) of Polish society. Consequently, the church has been successful in promoting what it calls cultural pluralism or a competing world view to that of the official state ideology. Such cultural pluralism, although individualized in Poland, nevertheless plays an important role in the life of Polish society.

It should be pointed out that the special role of the Roman Catholic Church in Poland is also due to the fact that a great many Poles regard religion as a political category rather than a purely spiritual one, emphasizing the church's association with national survival, culture, and continuity. In other words, the church is elevated in the popular consciousness to a symbol of Polishness and of resistance to a system perceived by many as dominated by foreign and historically hostile forces.

Recent studies undertaken by Polish sociologists tend to support these suggestions. The results of the research on industrializing regions indicate that while most Poles in these areas identify themselves as religious, their faith is not necessarily confirmed by such empirical tests as regular church attendance or depth of internalization of Christian values or norms. Moreover, the process of intense industrialization, especially during the 1970s, has led many to a deviation from the "model of traditional folk religion" (Piwowarski 1977, 10-40). The rate of neutrality towards religion has markedly increased while the level of Christian knowledge has decreased. Particularly in the area of "moral behavior," the questioning of Christian tenets has reached the level of over 50 percent of the respondents (ibid., 212). Yet there remains a high level of general identification with the church as a religious institution.

What appears to have emerged in Poland since the establishment of Communist rule is civil religion -- a pattern of symbols, ideas, and practices that legitimate the authority of civil institutions in society, particularly in the area of national values. Civil religion in this context is religious in that it evokes commitment and, within an overall world view, expresses a people's ultimate sense of worth, identity, and destiny; it is civil in that it deals with the basic public institutions exercising power in society. It manifests itself through ritual observances, holidays, sacred places, documents, stories, heroes, and in other ways. This quite clearly is the case in Poland, perhaps more than anywhere else in Eastern Europe. In the consciousness of Poles, religious and national values are an integrated and indivisible element of national culture.

As shown in a Polish sociological study (Kolarska and Rychard 1982, 216), the 1980s have brought significant popular support for the church's involvement in public life. Although support varied according to social status, it was overwhelming even among high-level managers (73 percent), while rank-and-file support reached still higher (86 percent). Interestingly, "non-allied" members of society (those not belonging to any political or union organization) attributed particular significance to the defensive, and hence socially crucial, role of the church (ibid.).

It should, however, be emphasized that the symbiosis of national, cultural, and democratic political traditions embodied in Polish Catholicism clearly reflects the church's own view of the nation and the state.

Nation and State in Polish Catholic Doctrine

Polish Catholic doctrine on nation and state combines the church's experience of its encounter with Communism in Poland and the social formulations of the Second Vatican Council (1962-1965) contained in the Pastoral Constitution on the Church in the World Today (Gaudium et spes), which declared the need to open the church to the social, economic, cultural and political problems of the world. According to the doctrine, the existence of a nation reflects the law of nature:

> Love for one's country, patriotism, is an important, inherited social virtue .... A nation is a different kind of reality from a state. It differs from a state because a nation is a communion of souls, it may exist, at least to a certain extent, independently from a territory and without its own state.
> (Jarocki 1964, 387)

The doctrine stresses that a nation is a community of specific ethical and cultural values: a heritage of work and creativity, of territory and political institutions, and of history and a specific historical consciousness. The last of these plays a particularly important role in this doctrine, because it integrates the national and religious ties. In order to function as an actor in history, a nation needs a certain ethical background, a moral course that is to be found in the nation's cultural heritage. This cultural heritage, which contains the essence of morality, lies at the root of all kinds of national ties. Religion, which embodies the national beliefs, is the kernel of the national culture. When religion dies, the national culture dies with it. The death of the nation must inevitably follow.

The church views the state, the natural association of people (societas naturalis), as the most important form of organization in the society. The task of the state is to work for the good of the community and to support the spontaneous activities of individuals and groups. The doctrine also stipulates the decentralized organization of the state and the functioning of several intermediary institutions between the individual and the state, including trade unions, local self-government, and self-management associations. Furthermore, it stresses that the political system should be the servant of the nation.

The foundation of this doctrine of nation and state is a hierarchy of values, with God and His creation--the human individual--at the top. Next is the nation and the development of its culture followed by the society together with conditions for free, spontaneous actions. At the bottom of the hierarchy is the state and its ability to fulfill its mission of serving the individual, the nation and the society. One of the most important consequences of the hierarchy is that it ascribes the role of the inspirer and adjudicator of the nation and the state to the church.

Pope John Paul II reiterated this doctrine in his sermon at Czestochowa during his second visit to Poland as follows:

> The nation is truly free when it can mould itself as a community determined by the unity of culture, language and history. The State is really sovereign if it governs the community serving at the same time the common good of society, and allows the nation to realize its own subjectivity, its own identity. Among other things this involves the creation of suitable conditions of development in the fields of culture, economics and other spheres of life of the social community. The sovereignty of the State is closely linked with the capacity to promote the freedom of the nation, that is to create conditions which will enable it to express the whole of its own historical and cultural identity, that means conditions which will allow it to be sovereign to the State.
> (Szajkowski 1983, 223)

The doctrine defines the parameters of the church's active engagement in all processes aimed at improving public life, including its engagement in politics. The latter, however, does not mean becoming a political partner in terms of formal politics. The church regards such political involvement as a process of competition for power, which is merely a temporary phenomenon. In its view, political parties and other social organizations, including trade unions, come and go -- the nation remains. In other words, social structures reflect only the current phase of the nation's development, a transitory aspect of man's work. The church, which embodies the nation's interest, must operate in a different dimension and time frame from those used by contemporary social groups. Therefore, while not denying the right of social groups to their own assessment of the situation and their own activity, the church must not become involved in a struggle among them. In a nutshell, the church's aspirations are above the purely political plane and are aimed primarily at the sovereign existence of Poland. Only when Polish sovereignty is guaranteed will the church again be able to safeguard and contribute effectively to the nation's intellectual, religious, and cultural traditions which are the basis for its development and expansion.

The church's doctrine on the nation and the state thus gives a unique insight into an understanding of its relations with civil society in Poland throughout the postwar period and in particular since the late 1960s.

The Locus of Civil Society in Poland

The reasons for the rebirth of civil society in Poland after three decades of established socialism are perhaps best summarized in a remarkable document, Report on the State of the Republic (Vale 1981), issued in May 1979 by a group of around one hundred people representing various academic disciplines and professions, including several members of the Central Committee of the PUWP. The report pointed out the lack of norms and rules in public life that could be generally accepted as operational by society at large, as well as the lack of general agreement on such fundamental matters as the conception of governing, the division of national income, and the evaluation of consequences resulting from Poland's geopolitical position. Furthermore, the report pointed to the political origins of the deep malaise affecting Polish society and singled out the lack of consensus between the rulers and they ruled on such important issues as national culture and history, private property, the legal system, and labor relations. In addition, the report stressed that the party leadership enjoyed exclusive privileges in the decision-making bodies while serving the interests of specific factions within the party rather than the needs of the society. The exclusion of broader segments of society from the mechanisms of power had resulted in a permanent loss of social support for the leadership. Moreover, the abuse of the legal system had seriously demoralized society, led to an explosion of corruption, and made it impossible to use legal rules and norms for the purposes of social mediation and economic management. Since the centralized party apparatus fully dominated the facade structures of the Sejm and the peoples' councils, there existed no system of institutionalized control over the activity of the government. Decision making was essentially regulated by the personal considerations of party officials. Thus the exercise of power and the management of the economy had become inefficient, ineffective, unrealistic, and incapable of self-correction.

The report gave a picture of a society deprived of

any right to express hopes or articulate designs for the actual creation of alternatives to the established ways of running its affairs. The document openly expressed what was known and felt by the majority of Poles--the decay of the political system, the loss of confidence, and the existence of an intellectual and political vacuum.

It was in this situation, between 1976 and the autumn of 1980, that numerous self-organized groups of social solidarity and cooperation sprang up in Poland outside the institutional framework of the state.* In addition, at least twenty <u>samizdat</u> papers with a total monthly circulation of not less than 30,000 began to appear regularly. Both these circumstances led to the self-organization of a plurality of interests outside the state in an increasingly independent social sphere --the civil society.

Conscious attempts at the constitution of civil society were undoubtedly accelerated by the election of Cardinal Karol Wojtyla as Pope John Paul II in October 1978 and his subsequent first papal visit to Poland. The accession of Cardinal Wojtyla to the papacy triggered an unprecedented demonstration of national and civic awareness. It was not just a religious event, but rather an event of national significance for Poland

---

*These included the following (date of formation in parentheses: Polish Youth Committee for the Implemittee for the Defense of Workers (September 1976); Movement for the Defense of Human Rights (March 1977); Student Solidarity Committee in Krakow (May 1977; in October 1977 Student Solidarity Committees were formed in Warsaw, Poznan, Wroclaw, Gdansk and Szczecin); the Democratic Movement (October 1977); Society for Academic Courses - commonly known as The Flying University (January 1978); the Katowice Committee for Free Trade Unions (February 1978); Committee for Free Trade Unions of the Baltic Seabord (April 1978); Lublin Region Farmers' Self-Defense Committee (July 1978); Grojec Region Farmers' Self-Defense Committee (September 1978); Committee for Free Trade Unions - Pomorze Region (October 1978); Rzeszow Region Farmers' Self-Defense Committee (November 1978); Believers' Self-Defense Committee - Podlasie Region (November 1978); The People's University (January 1979); Social Self-Defense Club (May 1979); The Peasant Center for Knowledge (June 1979); Center for People's Thought (July 1979); The Young Poland Movement - (July 1979); Believers' Self-Defense Committee Przemysl (August 1979); Confederation for Independent Poland (September 1979); Committee for National Self-Determination (September 1979); Believers' Self-Defense Committee - Cisow (December 1979); Independent Self-Governing Trade Union "Solidarity" (August 1980).

that gave a massive infusion of confidence to the self-organized opposition groups, particularly among young people.
 The papal visit was a psychological earthquake. The pope expressed in public what had been hidden for decades--the people's private hope and longing for uncensored truth, for dignity and courage in defense of their civil and human rights. His words gave them a sense of confidence, unity, and strength to take up their causes even more decisively. His visit demonstrated that after more than three decades of Communist rule and despite atheist indoctrination, the church was still an overwhelming power in the nation. Moreover, it rendered the role of the party less significant, showing that whatever its claims, the party was not the guiding force in the nation. The visit demonstrated once again what was already obvious: that the vast majority of the population had come to regard the Catholic Church, the only independent large-scale organization capable of standing up to the party, as a lobbyist through which to pursue the people's interests. The statute and role of the church thus demonstrated the inability of the regime to integrate society into the established patterns of party-dominated mass organizations.
 The visit became a powerful manifestation of the bond between the Polish people and the world of Christian culture, demonstrating their solidarity with the Catholic Church, their national pride in the person of Pope John Paul and their yearning for change, the symbol of which they saw in their countryman. The significance of this demonstration, expressed so spontaneously and vigorously, had a lasting effect on Poland, resulting in the maturing of historical processes sooner than most people had expected. The pope in his sermons caught the precise self-image of the Poles, into whom he injected new courage and a new desire for self-assertion. In view of this the party was obviously no longer in a position to arrest the evolution of independent social groups toward greater self-confidence.
 The direct impact of the first papal visit lay in strengthening of the organization of the civil society in terms of both its infrastructure and in the subsequent more overt articulation of demands vis-a-vis the state. After the pope's visit the church continued to increase its moral authority and standing in society, as well as its credibility and prestige in relation to state authorities, which increasingly had to take the church's views into account. Similarly, the church, having provided a focus for the expression of the aspirations of the civil society, also provided it with both the language and the mechanisms, of their articulation. It was increasingly viewed by both the self-organized groups and the state as an umbrella organiz-

ation for the elements of civil society in Poland. Needless to say, the church's position had been acquired as a result of its long history of determined actions in defense of civil society, a position that was further enhanced during the Solidarity period (August 1980 - December 1981) and that has remained essentially unchanged since the declaration of martial law on December 13, 1981. It should be remembered that the defense of civil society was and continues to be the <u>modus operandi</u> of the church's doctrinal view of the nation and the state.

The Church's Actions in Defense of Civil Society

Almost the entire history of church-state relations in People's Poland has been punctuated by the church's activities in support of elements of civil society (see Szajkowski 1983). For our purpose here it will be sufficient to summarize these actions under the following headings:
1. <u>Demands for respect of human and civil rights.</u> The church has consistently defended human and civil rights, stressing that man enjoys certain inviolable and inalienable rights not due to any grants from a government or community but due to the fact that he is a human being. These rights include not only freedom for workers, farmers, and students to organize their own independent trade union organizations, but also the right of society to social justice, free cultural activity, freedom of information including the abolition of censorship, and freedom of expression, including the right to express opinions on matters concerning public life.
2. <u>Demands for ending the state's monopoly over the education system.</u> This is based on the church's view that the official interpretation of Polish history taught in the schools and universities is based on the Marxist theory of class struggle and therefore neglects many of the values of the past that continue to be the objects of Polish national pride. Polish Catholicism which is professed by some 90 percent of the population, not only does not share such a critical appraisal of the past but on the contrary stresses traditional values and expresses the sovereignty of the nation in its history as a contemporary source for pride.
3. <u>Insistence on the harmful consequences of the domination of society by one group.</u> The church's view is that the ideology of the socialist welfare state is suitable to express only a few aspirations and that it reduces the human being and the citizen to the role of producer and consumer.
4. <u>Demands for the ending of repression.</u> These demands were made forcefully and continuously after the 1970 and 1976 workers' riots when the church condemned

the authorities for using violence and demanded the release of prisoners. Similar unequivocal demands were also made for the release of political prisoners during the 1970s and of both internees and political prisoners after the imposition of martial law in 1981. During that period the church also set up a system of legal advice centers for the victims of martial law and protested the loyalty pledges required of Solidarity members, by the military regime which was contrary to the Polish Constitution and to international agreements ratified by the Polish People's Republic. At the same time the Polish episcopate issued detailed instructions on what to do when such pledges were extracted forcibly.

5. <u>Mediation</u>. The church's considerable mediation efforts were not restricted to its well-documented actions during the closing stages of the strike in the Lenin Shipyard in August 1980, during the period preceding the legalization of Solidarity and Farmer's Solidarity (also known as Rural Solidarity), during the strikes in Bielsko Biala and the Bydgoszcz sit-in, and after the declaration of martial law. They also involved sending a letter by the pope to Leonid Brezhnev, as well as papal contact with Vladimir Zagladin, the CPSU Central Committee representative.

6. <u>Creation of institutions supporting elements of civil society</u>. The church created several institutions to support civil society, including the Primate's Committee on Trade Unions (August 1980), Committees for Help to Internees (December 1981) and the Primate's Social Council (December 1981). The last of these was responsible for issuing a series of documents for public discussion, including the theses in the "Matter of Social Accord" that suggested an imaginative way out of Poland's social and economic difficulties. The Council also formulated the basic framework for the Church's Recovery Program in aid of private farmers.

Finally, it should be pointed out that the church has continued to articulate its support for civil society in Poland through memoranda and written submissions to state authorities; it has also maintained direct contacts through the Joint Episcopal-Government Commission and periodic high-level meetings. Above all, however, this support is propagated and legitimized in public in pastoral letters and most importantly through the uncensored use of the church pulpit.

Conclusions

The strong links between the Roman Catholic Church and the institutions of civil society in Poland have been forged as a result of the church's consistent and determined actions on behalf of a social sphere independent of the hegemonic political and ideological structures of socialism. This sphere has remained remarkably resilient despite more than three decades of socialist rule, decades that have seen profound economic, social, political and ideological changes instituted by the party and the state. In contrast, the institutions of civil society have become more and more identified with the church and its own concept of the nation and the state. At the same time the church's defense of civil society has become the means of promoting its own special doctrine which, needless to say, is diametrically opposed to that of the Communist party and all the institutions controlled through "democratic centralism."

There is little doubt that the church as an institution has benefited from its relations with civil society as well as with the state. These benefits have been particularly evident in the church's unique opportunities to influence the state's decisions, which has given the church a privileged institutional position. At the same time it is also clear that the church has played a politically stabilizing role in Poland.

As Parkin (1972) has suggested, religious institutions may become politically radicalized when there are no other formal political outlets for the expression of a wide range of political, moral, and material grievances. This situation, as we see in Poland, can lead not only to the enrichment of the church's official doctrine, but can also contribute to stronger links between the organizational infrastructure of the church and the pluralistic structures created by the society.

REFERENCES

Althusser, Louis. 1963. For Marx. Hammondworth: Penguin.
Arato, Andrew. 1981. "Civil Society Against the State: Poland 1980-81." Telos 47 (Spring), 23-47.
Cohen, Jean L. 1983. Class and Civil Society: The Limits of Marxian Critical Theory. Oxford: Oxford University Press.
Engels, Frederick. 1973. "Ludwig Feuerbach and the End of Classical German Philosophy." In K. Marx and F. Engels, Selected Works. 3. Moscow: Progress Publishers.
Gramsci, Antonio. 1971. Selections from the "Prison Notebooks", Q. Hoare and P. Nowell Smith, eds. London: Lawrence and Wishart.
Hegel, G. W. F. 1965. Hegel's Philosophy of Right. Oxford: Oxford University Press.
Jakubowski, F. 1976. Ideology and Superstructure in Historical Materialism. London: Allison and Busby.
Jarocki, S. 1966. Katolicka nauka spoleczna (The Catholic Social Teaching). Paris: Societe d'Editions Internationales.
Kolarska, Lena and Andrzej Rychard. 1982. "Visions of Social Order." In W. Adamski et al., eds. Sisyphus 3. Warsaw: Polish Scientific Publishers.
Marx, Karl. 1973. "Preface to A Contribution to the Critique of Political Economy." K. Marx and F. Engels, Selected Works 2. Moscow: Progress Publishers.
──────. 1973. "The German Ideology." K. Marx and F. Engels, Selected Works 1. Moscow: Progress Publishers.
Miliband, Ralph. 1963. The State in Capitalistic Society. London: Weidenfeld and Nicholson.
Parkin, Frank. 1972. Class Inequality and Political Order. London.
Pastoral Constitution on the Church in the World Today (Gaudium et spes). 1969. London: Catholic Truth Society.
Piwowarski, Wladyslaw. 1977. Religijnosc miejska w rejonie uprzemy Slowionym. (Urban Religiosity in an Industrialized Area). Warsaw.
Poulantzas, Nicos. 1973. Political Power and Social Class. London: New Left Books.
──────. 1978. State, Power, Socialism. London: New Left Books.
Szajkowski, Bogdan. 1983. Next to God ... Poland: Politics and Religion in Contemporary Poland. London: Frances Pinter.

Urry, J.   1981.   The Anatomy of Capitalist Societies.
     London: Macmillan.
Vale, Michael. 1981. Poland: The State of the Republic. London: Pluto Press.

Part Two
BEYOND SOLIDARITY

6
Eastern Europe in the "Crisis of Transition": The Polish and Hungarian Cases
Robert Manchin and *Ivan Szelenyi*

The Nature of Socioeconomic Crisis in Eastern Europe

East European economists have long since ceased to believe that crises are exclusively a characteristic of market capitalism. Socialist countries may also experience crises, even if official textbooks on the political economy of socialism do not acknowledge that fact. Most economists understand that such vulnerability to crisis is not due simply to the impact of participation in the world market; they identify the inherent contradictions of the state socialist reproduction process as the source of socialist economic crisis.
"Crisis theory" has taken three main forms. The "cyclical crisis" theory developed by Bauer (1981) identified investment cycles as the functional equivalents of the overproduction cycles of capitalist economies (Kalecki 1972; Brody 1983). The crucial distinction between extensive and intensive growth was introduced by Janossy (1971), who argued that both capitalist and socialist economies pass through these stages and that socialist economies arrived at the transition point during the 1960s. He referred to this long structural crisis as the "crisis of transition." Finally, younger economists have argued that the present crisis is here to stay, since they seriously doubt that socialist economies can ever learn to cope with the tasks of intensive growth. Socialism, from this perspective, is a strategy for extensive industrialization, which becomes redundant when the industrialization phase ends. This theory of the "general crisis" of socialism does not subscribe to the belief that socialist economic systems can be reformed and assumes that sooner or later they will have to be abandoned.

The cyclical crisis of state socialist redistributive economies

Relying on rich empirical material from different East European economies, Bauer's theory (1981) argues that over the last three decades, one can clearly demonstrate cyclical fluctuations in state socialist economies. The source of these fluctuations is investment since it stimulates the economic cycle in state socialism. The early stages of the economic upturn are characterized by overheated investment, which results in overinvestment; this situation undermines economic dynamism and generates a downturn in the economy, which can only be resolved by drastic cutbacks in investments. The reduction consolidates government budgets, prepares the ground for a new upturn in the economy, and leads a new wave of overheated investment.

The role of underinvestment under state socialism is similar to that of overproduction under market capitalism. According to Kornai (1982, 1983), overinvestment in a socialist economy results from the absence of profit limits within the government budget. Since natural resources are the sole constraint within a bureaucratically coordinated economy, a socialist "business cycle" with too many unreasonable investments follows. Low governmental resistance to industrial pressures allows too many investments, while the low effectiveness of investments further contributes to the scarcity of capital, material, and manpower. At this point in the cycle, the central planning system intervenes by freezing some of the investment projects. Such intervention lowers investment effectiveness, since unfinished projects bring no immediate returns. Overinvestment derives from competition among redistributors for their share of state budgets. While under a capitalist economy profit maximization is achieved through competition between individual capitalists, resulting in cyclical overproduction, a redistributive economy maximizes the central budget by competition between redistributors for investment funds from state budgets, which also leads to overinvestment (Konrad and Szelenyi 1979; Szelenyi 1978; Polanyi 1957).

The concept of "investment cycles" is a major contribution to the political economy of state socialism, but it has its limitations, which is why the "crisis of transition" theory may have some explanatory value.

The theory of the crisis of transition

For East European economists the distinction between extensive and intensive stages of economic growth has been of vital importance in explaining the problems that state socialist societies began to face during the 1960s. In the East European context, extensive growth coincided with the socialist industrialization that followed World War II and ended during the 1960s. The term "extensive growth" can also be used to describe the stage in which a growing labor force makes a primary contribution to economic accomplishment. Capitalist economies experienced their extensive growth stage prior to the 1930s. At some point the sources of labor dried up. Abundant, cheap labor was no longer available, so the economy had to foster measures of intensive growth, relying not on the numerical growth of the labor force, but on increased productivity. Such a transformation of an economy required a new system of macroeconomic management to correspond with the qualitatively new mode of reproduction.

The shift from an extensive capitalist economy was followed by the Great Depression, the greatest economic crisis in the history of capitalism. The "crisis of transition" theory identified the Great Depression as a structural crisis that divided the two major phases in capitalist development for the last two hundred years. Two extreme strategies were employed to ease the traumatic transition of the economy into the intensive mode. In Nazi Germany the economy was militarized to keep individual consumption and income at a low level. It made a high demand on the means of production through state military expenditures. In the United States the "New Deal" strategy was employed to stimulate demand on the means of production. It was achieved through increased individual consumption, which stimulated general economic development. Recently, the American economy has combined state military expenditures with a high level of individual consumption, supplementing the economic market by a subordinate redistributive sector, primarily in the welfare area.

The crisis of transition experienced by East European countries in the 1960s resulted from the exploitation of labor resources by the industrial sector. Since extensive growth ended (in Czechoslovakia in the early 1950s, in East Germany, Hungary and Poland in late 1970s), socialist economies have slipped into a crisis, producing very low, frequently negative growth rates and a stagnation in the living standards of the population. Eastern Europe thus entered a structural (as opposed to cyclical) crisis, as a result of the transition to the intensive growth stage. As in the case of capitalism, a successful transition would require new modes of economic reproduction and a new economic management system. As under capitalism, two extreme strategies are possible: the militarization of the economy and/or the promotion of mass consumption. The strategy of militarizing the economy, if effectively imposed by an arms race with the West, would suppress the promotion of mass consumption, opening the way to increased power for the Communist party-state bureaucracy.

The mode of extensive growth in socialist economies has favored rigid central planning and the monopoly of bureaucratic redistributive coordination, so that the needs of consumers have been effectively suppressed (Feher et al. 1983). While a similar management system may be maintained if the militarization of the economy is the strategy chosen to cope with the transition, the alternative strategy, that of mass consumption, would require the abolition of command measures. A socialist economy, if based on promoted consumption, would also become a mixture of market mechanisms (regarding individual consumption) and redistributive mechanisms (regarding collective consumption and welfare). Increased consumer autonomy would result, reflecting the increasing autonomy of a civil society liberating itself from the tutelage of the political state; political and civil liberties would be considerably extended.

The transition to such an intensive stage is not easy, since it may be vigorously resisted by redistributors with vested interests in maintaining their monopoly. Such a transition could even be a turning point for the system, since it might revert to capitalism, move toward militarization of the economy within a neo-Stalinist political structure, or evolve toward democratic socialism or socialism with a "human face."

The theory of the general crisis of socialism

Since no analysis of the general crisis of socialism is available in the literature to date, a summary of interviews with young Hungarian economists (conducted in the summer of 1983) follows. They rejected the crisis of transition on three counts: first, the redistributive economy is not an adequate system for the task of extensive growth; second, the idea of transition to intensive growth is an illusion; and third, the long world recession of the 1970s produced structural changes in countries peripheral to the West, while nothing comparable occured in Eastern Europe. As a result, Eastern Europe is losing its position on the semiperiphery of the world economic system, and moving towards the periphery. Socialism is currently undergoing a general crisis, because it consistently produces zero growth and because living standards have decreased since the late 1970s without subsequent modernization of the economy. Exchange relationsips with capitalist countries have deteriorated and have been followed by a legitimation crisis.

The theory of the general crisis does not imply the automatic collapse of socialism. It foresees instead a bleak future for the economy, which would settle at a low level, locked into a vicious circle of low productivity and low quality. Subsequently, socialist countries would trade with each other

products that are usable but unsalable on the world market. Such an economy can keep going indefinitely if sufficient technical innovation is guaranteed in the military area.
This gloomy picture cannot be dismissed out of hand. Only history can prove which of the above theories is correct. Although a general crisis of socialism is possible, the reform potential of East European economies is not yet exhausted and an intensive socialist economy is feasible. The redistributive economy has achieved some level of extensive growth without private ownership and profit incentives, but this will not suffice to move socialist economies from the semiperiphery to the center. Further intensive growth, as illustrated by the case of Hungarian agriculture, is possible only if a mixed mode of production is achieved.

Strategies of Transition

During the 1960s two strategies were worked out to cope with the crisis of transition and to create an intensive socialist economy. In East Germany the emphasis was on the rationalization of central planning and redistribution, while in Hungary a combination of decentralized decision making and market mechanisms was enforced (Nove 1979). Other East European countries then chose one of these two strategies or a mix of both to suit their domestic conditions. The way in which the Soviet Union will face the crisis of transition is particularly important for the future of Eastern Europe. The paradox of European socialist development is that the Soviet satellites are economically more advanced than the Soviet Union itself. The Soviet Union is a latecomer to the crisis of transition. In the 1960s proponents of both the East German and Hungarian strategies began a reform movement in the U.S.S.R., but it eventually withered away. The fact that the Soviet Union is lagging behind economically has had negative consequences, since it has not felt the necessity to find a solution to the crisis of transition. Soviet leaders curb experiments, as seen in Czechoslovakia and Poland, before the value of such experiments can ever be assessed. Soviet domination of Eastern Europe will therefore delay the process of transition.

The East German strategy

The central idea of the East German model seems to be that there is nothing inherently wrong with central planning and redistribution. The idea that a scientific-technical revolution would get Eastern Europe out of trouble was common in the mid-1960s. Radovan Richta and his reformist circle advocated this approach in Czechoslovakia as an alternative to a more radical structural reform. East Germany, unlike Czechoslovakia, had some limited success in implementing this idea. During the 1970s East Germany claimed to rank among the top economic powers in Europe, with a stable per capita income, making it exceptional among other East European countries. This was achieved without inflation or increased social inequalities, which were the by-products of the Hungarian model. The East German model thus had some success; at any rate, the idea of a scientific-technical revolution certainly appealed to segments of the technical intelligentsia. The work of Bahro (1978), which stressed scientific planning and the intelligentsia's decisive role in running the economy, shows this. The conservatism of the East German scientific-technical solution is obvious in light of the fact that the party-state bureaucracy has conserved its power monopoly, giving only minor concessions to the technical intelligentsia. When evaluating the success of the East German model, one should not forget, however, that the economy was nourished by West Germany, which sought civil and political concessions from the East German government in return for economic aid. The East German regime has nevertheless experienced increasing legitimation problems and its economic indicators show a slowdown.

Post-New Deal developments in the West indicate that an intensive economy requires mixed forms of economic coordination. The transition to the intensive stage cannot be achieved simply by upgrading redistribution. Whereas the transition in the West required that the dominant market mechanism be complemented by redistribution, in the East such a transition would require that the dominant redistributive sector be complemented by market mechanisms.

The Hungarian model

The Hungarian model, initiated in the mid-1960s as an economic reform, allowed increasing market coordination while the state retained some hegemony over planning and redistributive measures. The hegemony over redistributive mechanisms meant that the dynamics of extended reproduction were controlled by central planning, the levels of employment and income were determined by central directives, and foreign trade remained under the control of the state apparatus.

The state apparatus thus retained its ability to allocate investment funds, to refuse to bargain over wage increases, and to control the world trade's impact on the domestic economy. Therefore, two critical areas for the socialist economy--allocation of labor and allocation of investments--remained under governmental redistributive control.

Simultaneously, however, several regulations concerning employment in agriculture, services and industrial production were gradually lifted during the 1970s, clearing the way for a second economy in which market mechanisms were allowed to work freely. Although such "marketization" appeared mostly on the peripheries of the Hungarian economy, in the early 1980s a considerable proportion (about 70 percent) of all families was receiving some income from activities in the second economy.

Extensively increased productivity and individual income stimulated an unprecedented supply of consumer goods and services, giving the impression of a mass consumption socialist society. Unlike the earlier Yugoslavian experience of the 1960s, the Hungarian model did not allow democratization or marketization of industrial relations on the shop floor. Instead of political concesions, as in Yugoslavia, Hungarian workers were offered only economic concessions.

Although economically successful, the Hungarian model is acclaimed mostly for its political accomplishments. It has allowed a complex class compromise, in which various layers of society have been given an economic share by the party-state system. Based on their experience in the 1956 revolution, the intellectuals have not called for radical politicoeconomic reforms, nor have party bureaucrats attempted any such reforms. A relatively high level of political stability has been retained throughout the 1970s and early 1980s, during which time Poland has been shattered by the legitimation crisis. Despite its limitations, however, the majority of economic demands articulated in 1956 have gradually been granted during the 1970s.

Political concessions, although excluded from the settlement with workers, were offered to the technical intelligentsia, which was allowed to play an increasing role in industrial management. In return for loyalty or political apathy, intellectuals enjoyed an impressive degree of tolerance and liberty, which made possible the appearance of previously unacceptable works (Konrad and Szelenyi 1979). The increased cross-class involvement of society in the second economy, combined with increased though still limited intellectual freedom, contributed to the dissolution of class conflict and eased the antagonisms between redistributors and direct producers. Consequently, Hungarian workers have been interested in neither labor unions nor wage levels. Labor in the redistributive sector has been treated as a compulsory service delivered to the master state in exchange for the freedom offered by the second economy. Political liberalism has resulted in a certain degree of loyalty and satisfaction among the people, as well as the legitimation of the state. At the cost of limited political liberty, economic autonomy, and material affluence, the party-state has obtained a considerable degree of overall stability and the possibility of retaining its control over crucial redistributive domains.

A civil society has emerged in Hungary that follows the classical pattern of capitalist societies elsewhere in the world. Crucial to this process has been the increased economic autonomy offered to the individual by the state. Socialist embourgeoisement, although denying several political liberties traditionally associated with a developed civil society and citizenship, has affected mostly the working class. In this way economic autonomy has emerged before parliamentary democracy, much the way that civil society developed in the West. From this perspective, the Polish strategy for creating a civil society appears as unusual, since the struggle was conducted at the political level before economic autonomy was achieved.

Despite its successes, the Hungarian model is not without contradictions. One of its important weaknesses is that a sizable proportion of the working class still does not benefit from the second economy, but is affected by the resulting inflation. In fact, approximately one third of the population remains outside of the second economy. Among the several social layers outside the second economy, three are of utmost importance: the retired, the disabled and the non-working poor; the traditional labor aristocracy--highly skilled heavy industry workers, who had been materially rewarded under the redistributive system; and the party-state bureaucracy, which has experienced not only a limitation of power, but also now earns considerably less than peasant workers.

Another shortcoming of the Hungarian model is that the willingness of the party-state bureaucracy to grant further concessions is limited. The bureaucracy is divided; while certain groups are willing to compromise as long as they can retain political monopoly, other factions clearly believe that the regime has already granted too many concessions. The presence of conservative forces was particularly visible during the 1972-1975 period, when an ouvrierist campaign against the 1968 reforms was launched by the leadership of the trade unions. Their position was that working-class and peasant income differences had been altered in favor of the latter group. The threat of economic anarchy, which would allegedly be brought about by a free market, led eventually to prohibitive legislation, that limited individual involvement in the second economy. This counterattack collapsed in 1975, when peasant-workers responded to the reintroduction of administrative regulations by decreasing production; this in turn resulted in significant increases in food prices. The Polish crisis has brought about a revitalization of ouvrierist opposition to the second economy. Party hard-liners have attempted to create a coalition between workers who do not benefit from the second economy and the conservative party bureaucrats.

Finally, another shortcoming of the Hungarian model stems from the dissatisfaction of intellectuals about the scope of concessions granted to them. The introduction of the second economy has delayed reform within the "first" (i.e. central) economic sector and within the political sphere. According to some economists (Brody 1983, Bauer 1982), a new reform is imminent, which would increase the power of technocracy at the factory level. The proponents of this reform see it as an alternative scheme for the allocation of investment goods, which would remove decision making from the control of the central bureaucracy and transfer this power to the hands of newly created holdings. As of mid-1984 there is still no consensus in Hungary; the social, political, and class struggles continue while the intelligentsia works out blueprints for socioeconomic reform.

The Unfolding of the Crisis in Poland. Is There a Hungarian Solution to the Polish Problems?

Defeat of the reform intelligentsia in 1968

The evolution of the reform movement in Poland and the decline of its economy into a crisis of transition resemble the developments in Hungary in the mid-1960s, when the intelligentsia was pressuring the party-state bureaucracy for concessions in marketing and decision making. Although some compromise was achieved in Hungary in 1968, Polish (and Czech) intellectuals suffered a major defeat, which had far-reaching consequences for future sociopolitical developments in Eastern Europe. While in Czechoslovakia the bureaucrats had to be protected by Warsaw Pact troops, Polish conservatives were stronger domestically. Reinforced by anti-Semitism, the government was able to mobilize working-class support and to defeat the proponents of reforms.

A massive intellectual exodus and the silencing of those who remained in the country had disastrous consequences for the entire economic system. With the intellectuals eliminated from the political scene, even the most effective, strategy would not work, since those power were able to generate enough support from the technocratic intelligentsia. Under these circumstances, the Hungarian model was not an option on the political agenda. Subsequently, Czechoslovakia entered a long period of bureaucratic counterrevoultion. In Poland, by contrast, Gomulka's departure helped retain some popular support for the party-state. The bureaucracy made a final, desperate attempt to show that it could lead society into the intensive stage of growth by exploiting the inherent potential of a redistributive economy with neither technocratic support, nor market reform.

"Second Poland" and the failure of the intensive growth strategy

In December 1970, a new leadership seized power in Poland and it appeared that it would move ahead with reform progrms. In 1973 an economic reform was introduced similar to the Hungarian project. In practical terms, however, this reform never accomplished a major transformation of the economic system, because the attempt to change the management system was overcautious and was sabotaged by local bureaucrats. The sole effect was a politically motivated increase in wages, aimed at defusing popular discontent. But this only fueled inflation and was insufficient to move the economy toward the intensive state. By the mid-1970s the regime abandoned even the mildest attempts at reform and a rebureaucratization of the economy got under way (Hare and Wanless 1981).

While his record with Hungarian-style reform is not impressive, Gierek should be commended for attempting a Polish experiment for intensive growth distinct from either of the earlier East European strategies. The essence of the Polish experiment was to borrow heavily from the West, invest these loans under strict redistributive control, and thus create a new industrial capacity, that would be competitive on the world market. The first stage of industrialization in Poland (the extensive one, accomplished under Gomulka's leadership in the 1950s and 1960s) was achieved at the expense of surplus labor drawn from agriculture. Unlike his predecessor, Gierek attempted to accomplish both increased industrial productivity and integration with world markets with neither substantial market reform nor improvements in the planning process. The collapse of this strategy was inevitable since it offered no structural changes or new incentives for more productive work.

The effects of the collapse of Poland's intensive growth strategy included the increased state monopoly of redistributive powers, a system of "soft" budgetary limits, and the waste of foreign loans. These developments illustrate why the Wallersteinian analysis of

East European economies is misleading. Wallerstein, subscribing to the theory of one capitalist world system, has suggested that socialist economies, after a short period of autarky, were reintegrated into the system of which they now form an integral part. Most progressive East European economists have argued instead that the problem is that socialist economies remain isolated from the international division of labor. The collapse of the Polish economy and the systematic way in which foreign loans were wasted prove Wallerstein wrong (see Wallerstein 1978).

The inevitability of the Polish model's collapse is further supported by the Hungarian experience; there too investment efficiency was very low. The spectacular spending on the petrochemical and steel industries turned out to be failures. Hungarians, however, also invested foreign funds in the production of consumer goods for the domestic market, which helped both the second economy and agriculture to expand and rescued the economic system from total collapse. The collapse of the Polish strategy should be seen as an inherent feature of Polish economic structure, not solely as the result of subjective mistakes by central planners. It should also be seen as implying the possible failure of the East German strategy, which has lacked substantial social compromise.

By the beginning of 1980 the regime in Poland was in a desperate situation. The totalitarian ending of the 1968 uprising had produced an intellectual crisis, which alienated or silenced a traditional source of reform: the intelligentsia. A stubborn bureaucracy systematically denied any concessions to the working class, technocrats, or the market economy, while the crisis of transition worsened. The absence of a viable strategy to cope with such a crisis was evident.

At this point, in August 1980, the working class attempted to initiate qualitatively new reform programs—a move unprecedented in a state socialist country. Although the events of 1980-1981 cannot be explained solely in class terms or in terms of the struggle surrounding the transition from an extensive to intensive model of growth, such a class analysis is facilitated by the triple character of Solidarity. It was first, a national movement, expressing Polish patriotism, particularly against Soviet domination; second, an ideological movement, opposing Communist totalitarianism with the values of Christianity and democracy; and third, a class movement, initiated and, to some extent, led by the working class. Born of the workers' resistance, the Solidarity movement was shaped largely by the workers, using intellectual advisers. During the subsequent stages of the movement's development (see chapter 1 of this volume), its working-class leadership retained a considerable degree of autonomy, despite becoming a cross-class organization. The workers' reservations were best expressed by Walesa in an interview with Oriana Fallaci: "Intellectuals need a lot of time to understand things, and even more to make a decision. They stay there to discuss ... and in five hours they reach the same conclusions I reached in five minutes" (Walesa 1981). As noted by Svitak (1981, 111), the existence of rank-and-file pressure and the fact that leadership remained in the hands of the workers distinguished the Polish revolution from the earlier Hungarian and Czechoslovak experiences. The workers' central role in the Polish revolution left its imprint on the nature of the political and economic reform programs that gradually appeared by the fall of 1981.

The slow pace at which reform demands were articulated was another feature of development in Poland that differentiates it from the Hungarian and Czech uprisings. In Hungary and Czechoslovakia the reformers offered articulated, detailed scenarios for change, but Solidarity did not have a reform program (either political or economic) and for several months it refused to participate in working out such a program. By mid-1981 the situation had changed drastically, once the Emergency Party Congress revealed that the party-state bureaucracy was unable and unwilling to initiate comprehensive and realistic reforms. Even during its own national convention in September 1981, the movement did not have a consistent reform scenario, remaining unable to make a choice between "Friedmanite" and social democratic programs. While the former suggested that productive capacities be transferred from the state to private ownership, the latter called only for "socialization" of the planning process (Ost 1981). The inability to make a choice may be interpreted as both a weakness, and a strength. Put simply, the movement's leadership refused to replace one elitist scenario with another emphasizing the necessity for negotiations between those in power and the entire society.

In this way, a new philosophy of the social contract was born. It proposed that an accord be reached among the state (as owner of the means of production), trade unions (organizations of workers as co-owners of the means of production), and self-management bodies, (organizations of workers as employees). Such a tripartite vision of the social order prevented Solidarity from trying to seize power, which might lead to new oppression. Solidarity instead claimed the right to co-own and comanage the system, without dismantling existing democratic institutions. Its aim was to create a permanent dual power system, with effective power sharing between the "owner state," "expert planners," (or rational redistributors), and the workers as direct producers, consumers, and citizens. This new conception of political and economic democracy emerged

directly under working-class influence.
Solidarity's gradually emerging reform program had yet another proletarian component--egalitarianism. Unlike intellectual programs, which are usually non-egalitarian (Csikos-Nagy 1984, 12-13), the Polish movement proclaimed the need for overall equality, thus differing from earlier Czech and Hungarian models and from the political practices of Gierek's government. This slow process, had it succeeded, would have contributed a new model of reform in Eastern Europe. Confronted with the threat of qualitatively new socialism on the one hand and the inability to produce a liberal power elite on the other, the party-state bureaucracy called for a military solution.
This political strategy, drawing heavily from the Kadarist tradition, was designed to use the military in the absence of a cooperative, technocratic intelligentsia, to modernize the system. So far, the military regime, strengthened by martial law, has failed to achieve any of its original objectives. It has dealt too tolerantly with the party-state bureaucracy and too harshly and oppressively with Solidarity to achieve even a surrogate social compromise.

The hope for a "Polish Model" for Eastern Europe

Despite the frustrating failures of the last few years--the failure to break the deadlock, to revive the economy, to achieve a social compromise, to reestablish the legitimacy of the regime--we still believe that the "cause of reform" and the transition to an intensively growing democratic socialism is far from lost. Particularly in contrast with Czechoslovakia, Poland seems to offer more hope for those who search for a solution of the East European structural crisis.
The most promising feature of the Polish situation is undoubtedly the strength of its civil society. (see Arato 1981). The existence of such a strong civil society has had its effect even on the martial law regime. In many respects this martial law regime was a curious one, for if Solidarity was a "self-limited revolution," this was in some sense a "self-restricted" martial law. For those familiar with the ruthlessness of the dictatorship in Hungary after the suppression of the 1956 uprising, it is difficult to comprehend how the military regime rejected "formal law." The regime was unable to respond to the "strike of the televisions" (in which people put their television sets in windows, protesting against manipulated, distorted news), was unable to "find" the underground Solidarity activists, and so on. This was martial law imposed on a highly developed civil society, on people with a heightened consciousness of citizenship and civil

rights; this martial law had to take these facts into account and compromise with them. Since martial law, Polish civic consciousness is very much alive, as one can see in the repeated pro-Solidarity demonstrations and the current "War of the Crosses" that has no precedent elsewhere in East Europe.

Therefore, we conclude that there is no Hungarian solution to the Polish crisis. The unfolding of the crisis in Poland proves that in Eastern Europe history does not repeat itself. Students of East European affairs attempted to predict what should have happened in Poland by drawing parallels with Hungary or Czechoslovakia, but the alternative of martial law could not have been inferred from the history of any country in the region. Yet once again, scholars seek historical examples: will Poland now follow the Hungarian pattern by reconsolidating itself in a Kadarist fashion or will it fall into the Czech style of bureaucracy? The military regime seems to believe in the possibility of achieving a solution based on the "Hungarian model".

In the final analysis, the Hungarian model is unlikely to work for Poland at the present time. After Solidarity, with the Catholic Church behind it and with the people's heightened "civic consciousness," it is hard to see how the second economy type of concessions could replace the program of "dialogue" and the "new social contract" for the Polish working class. It is also difficult to see how the technical intelligentsia could be won over by the regime without dialogue or a "new social contract."

Ten years after the defeat of the Hungarian revolution, the key demands of the revolution were reinstated in the political agenda, and social compromise was achieved. The Hungarian model emerged as these demands were met. It is possible, therefore, that in the coming years the key demands of Solidarity will also be reinstated in the political agenda and a "Polish model" of compromise will emerge. The essence of such a model would be the integration of economic, social and political reform, a model in which the autonomy of civil society is not limited to the economic sphere, as it is in the current "Hungarian model," but in which the notion of citizenship gains both political and social meaning.

REFERENCES

Arato, Andrew. 1981. "Civil Society Against the State, Poland 1980-1981." Telos 47 (Spring).
_____. 1982. "Empire vs. Civil Society." Telos 50 (Winter 1981-82).
Bahro, Rudolf. 1978. The Alternative in Eastern Europe. London: New Left Books.
Bauer, Tamas. 1981. Tervgazdasag, Beruhazas, Ciklusok. (Planned Economy, Investments, Cycles). Budapest: Kozgazdasagi es Jogi.
_____. 1982. "A mosodik gazdasagi reform es a tulajdonviszonyok." (The Second Economic Reform and Property Relations). Mozgo Vilag 11.
_____. 1983. "The Hungarian Alternative to Soviet-type Planning." Journal of Comparative Economics 3.
Brody, Andras. 1983 "A gazdasagi mechanizmus biralatanak harom hullama." (The Three Waves of Criticisms of the Economic Mechanism). Kozgazdasagi Szemle 7-8.
Csikos-Nagy, Bela. 1984. "Tis kerdes a gazdasagpolitikankrol." (Ten Questions About Our Economic Policy). Valosag 4.
Feher, Ferenc, Agnes Heller, and Gyorgy Markus. 1983. Dictatorship over Needs London: Basil Blackwell.
Galeski, Boguslaw. 1982. "Social Structure--Conflicts of Interests--Social Forces in Poland". Sisyphus 3 Warsaw: Polish Scientific Publishers.
Hare, T. Wanless. 1981. "Polish and Hungarian Economic Reforms--a Comparison." Soviet Studies (October).
Janossy, Ferenc. 1971. "Gazdasagunk mai ellentmondasainak eredete es felszamolasuk utja." (Origins of and Solutions to the Current Contradictions of our Economy). Kozgazdasagi Szemle 7-8.
Kalecki, Michal. 1972. "Introduction to the Theory of Growth in a Socialist Economy". Selected Essays on Economic Growth of a Socialist and Mixed Economy. Cambridge: Cambridge University Press. (first published in Polish in 1963).
Konrad, Gyorgy and Ivan Szelenyi. 1979. The Intellectuals on the Road to Class Power. New York: Harcourt, Brace and Jovanovich.
Kornai, Janos. 1980. Economics of Shortage. Amsterdam: North-Holland.
_____. 1983. "Burokratikus es piaci koordinacio." (Bureaucratic and Market Coordination). Kozgazdasagi Szemele 9.
Kovacs, Janos Matyas. 1984. "A reformalku surujeben". (The Process of "Reform-bargain"). Valosag 3.

Kurczewski, Jacek. 1982. "The Old System and the Revolution." Sisyphus 3 Warsaw: Polish Scientific Publishers.
Nove, Alec. 1979. "The Politcs of Economic Reform". A. Nove, ed. Political Economy and Soviet Socialism. London: Allen & Unwin,
Nove, Alec, et al. 1982. The East-European Economies in the 1970s. London: Allen & Unwin.
Pankow, Wlodzimierz. 1982. "The Roots of 'The Polish Summer': A Crisis of the System of Power". Sisyphus 3 Warsaw: Polish Scientific Publishers.
Peter, Gyorgy. 1956. A gazdasagossag es jovedelmezoseg jelentosege a tervgazdalkodasban. (The Significance of Rentability and Profitability in Planned Economies). 1/2 Budapest: Kozgazdasagi es Jogi.
Polanyi, Karl. 1957. "The economy as instituted process." K. Polanyi. Trade and Market in Early Empires. Glencoe, Ill.: Free Press.
Richta, Radovan and collective. 1969. Civilization at the Crossroads. Prague: International Arts and Sciences Press.
Sodaro, Michael and Sharon Wolchik, eds. 1983. Foreign and Domestic Policy in Eastern Europe in the 1980s. New York: St. Martin's Press.
Svitak, Ivan. 1981. "Comparison." Telos 47 (Spring).
Szego, Andrea. 1983. "Erdek es gazdasagi intezmenyrendszer." (Interests and Economic Institutions). Valosag 6.
_____. 1983. "Gazdasag es politika - erdek es struktura." (Economy and Politics - Interests and Structure). Medyetanc 2-3.
Szelenyi, Ivan. 1978. "Social Inequalities in State Socialist Redistributive Economies." International Journal of Comparative Sociology 1-2.
Tardos, Marton. 1982. "Program a gazdasagiriranyitas es a szervezeti rendszer fejlesztesere." Kozgazdasagi Szemle 6.
_____. 1983. "Reform: itt es most?" (Reform: Here and Now?) Mozgo Vilag 2.
Wallerstein, Immanuel. 1978. "Semi-peripherical Countries and the Contemporary World Crisis." I. Wallerstein, ed. The Capitalist World Economy. New York: Cambridge University Press.

7
The State and the Legitimacy Crisis
Barbara A. Misztal

Contemporary social movements in East and West have once again put democracy and democratization on their banners. (Arato and Goldfarb 1983, 705)

Of the several theoretical perspectives on socialist society, some emphasize similarities to the capitalist system, while others stress divergences from it. The most recent perspective views the uniqueness of socialist society as resulting from the fact that political control dominates its economic life. The main debate therefore concerns the nature of political and economic rule under socialism.

Analyses of capitalism are more advanced. It is no longer adequate, however, to analyze the two systems without reference to each other and to the type of state in particular. The issues of democracy and democratization of state systems, which are most significant for the immediate future of societies, especially require such a broadening of the theoretical perspective. The transition to a more democratic system has to be faced by each type of society, regardless of its specific problems. The process of transition to more democratic forms of social life brings about rifts and crises encountered by both types of societies.

The analyses of such crises, although dealing separately with capitalist and socialist societies, have one feature in common: they focus on the state and social movements. This article represents an attempt to understand the crisis within contemporary states by emphasizing the pressure exerted by social movements to force bureaucratic and irrational state apparatuses to loosen their control and diminish their domination over societies.

The Crisis of Legitimacy: Class Conflict at the Ideological Level

The problem of legitimacy is identified by several authors as the key to the contradictions and conflicts occurring within advanced capitalism. According to Habermas (1973), the decay of legitimacy stems from the normative basis of the capitalist system. Following the end of liberalism, changes in the market and within the economy have made governmental intervention the only way in which capitalism can be sustained. Politics directly penetrates the economy, causing the repoliticization of the institutional framework of society (ibid., 37). Irrational decisions of the administrative system follow, as a consequence of the shift of the fundamental contradiction of capitalism from the economic into the political system. The unresolved problems have a dysfunctional impact on the dominant bourgeois ideology, while the expansion of state activity in the economic sphere increases the need for legitimation (ibid., 36).

The demystification and collapse of bourgeois ideology, as well as growing popular expectations, make "the hand of the state" more visible and intelligible than the "invisible hand" of the liberal state. The range of social life seen by the general population as politicized or subject to potential governmental control subsequently increases (Held 1983, 493). With the expansion of state activity, its role becomes more apparent, and there is danger of further exposure to its nondemocratic nature and protectionism toward capitalist interests. Confronted with state activisim, popular feelings are stimulated toward an expectation of more protection for society. This is enough to stir a legitimacy crisis within the existing economic and political order. "In the final analysis, class structure is the source of the legitimation deficit" (Habermas 1976, 73). Society, facing the state's inability to produce legitimation, attempts to overcome the crisis by organizing itself according to the new principle of "a universalistic morality embedded in a system of participatory democracy" (Held 1983, 426). The need for a new motivation pattern (or normative consensus), and a new form of societal representation may overcome class contradictions and the crisis of capitalist state.

Following Habermas (1976), one can point to the role of the advanced capitalist state in the domain of the economy as a direct cause of a legitimacy crisis. In the attempt to displace the class conflict from the economy and to maintain social equilibrium, state interventionism heightens popular expectations. At the same time, however, the state's administrative system becomes increasingly irrational. Subsequently, the state is perceived as taking unequal care of various citizens' and groups' interests. It becomes instead the locus of antagonism within the civil society. While initially the state may have been able to absorb and regulate social conflicts, its increased intervention limits the state's ability to provide political solutions to economically generated problems. Interventionism thereby undermines the process of private accumulation, which the state would ordinarily protect as essential to capitalist reproduction (Offe 1975).

The restructuring of the power balance between the forces of labor and business that results from the dynamics of capital accumulation further limits state activity. "It is this asymmetry between labor and capital which constantly tends to disrupt the empirical consensus necessary for the viable functioning of ad-hoc, non-constitutional corporatist mechanisms of decision-making" (Offe 1984, 186). Decreasing stability and diminishing popular acceptance of the sociopolitical order result from the absence of consensus as to legitimate ways of solving basic contradictions. The centralization and bureaucratization of the polity sphere further exclude various social layers from the possibility of articulating their interests or questioning the existing relationships between polity and society. Subsequently, the normative foundations of the liberal democratic arrangements are also questioned. In this situation new social movements emerge.

The Conflict Between the Socialist State and Civil Society

The concept of legitimacy has been used by several students of the 1980-1984 period in Poland (Pankow, 1982; Staniszkis 1982). They presupposed that one could comprehend the crisis through an analysis of the popular perception of the socialist state. They also also believed that increasing state control and responsibility for welfare provisions heightened the system's need for legitimacy. From this perspective, the Polish crisis is related to the breakdown in the legitimacy of the state. Following the Weberian typology of the legitimacy of political orders, some authors have indicated a similarity between the crisis in Poland and the crisis caused by a lack of traditional legitimacy (Jasinska 1983). As pointed out by Jasinska, "the belief in the inviolability and immutability of a given order" and the idea that "no alternative to it can be conceived" (1983, 161) place such interpretations within the Weberian concept of traditional legitimacy. Other approaches, however, point to the similarity between the Polish situation and the "rationality crisis" as explained by Habermas, in which the administrative system fails to produce the required number of rational decisions (ibid.).

The structure of argumentation is common to these two approaches and can be reconstructed in the following way. The legitimation process in Poland encountered several constraints from the beginning of the Communist rule in 1944. The implementation of the new political system after World War II was dubious from the legal point of view; its public approval was fictitious. Since "revolutions are not necessarily illegitimate," however, and since they can establish a pattern of order that "supercedes legitimacy of the former regime" (Strenberger 1968, 244), the absence of political legitimacy did not rule out the chances of the Communist ruling group to pursue some successful social changes. The official ideology, as the main safeguard of the socialist system, emphasized the inviolability of political order and stressed functional and future-oriented techniques (Pankow 1982). Its legitimacy was thus rooted in the premise of a "better tomorrow" that was to be achieved by means of the Communist system. The rulers attempted to legitimize their power through demonstrations of their ability to produce a society of satisfied consumers (Lewis 1982). Such an ideology stimulated demands, raised societal aspirations, and made highly visible the discrepancy between reality and the vision displayed and produced by the polity. As Pankow has noted:

> In a system of power in which the dominant legitimation is functional in nature, that is such which refers to human needs and interests, social cooperation--the principal and practically the only source of values and goods which can satisfy those needs and interests--becomes indirectly the fundamental condition of the faith in the legitimation of the authorities (hence also of its de facto legitimation), while the authorities themselves determine the chances of correct social cooperation (1982, 38).

The decrease in the system's economic efficiency thus resulted from the absence of democratic mechanisms. Subsequently, the center of political power gradually lost its ability to attain the objectives of the official ideology. The sociopolitical crises in postwar Poland continually revoked and re-created social approval as the basis for legitimacy. By its involvement in the crisis, civil society has learned that the "bureaucratic structures and the system of power behind them are incapable of changing their policies without social pressure extended upon them" (Morawski 1982, 7). From the stage where the "empirical attitudes of trust and satisfaction are disturbed by the system's failure to function," society has advanced to the next stage, where a feeling develops that the system does not work according to its own established standards (Offe 1984, 172). Offe's analysis of the legitimacy crisis can be applied to the situation in Poland, in which social consciousness became broadened and liberalized beyond the limits set by the polity. Previously unheard-of political activities, such as strikes, underground publishing, and political defiance, became a part of regular social life. Subsequently, the state's presence in economic and cultural life decreased, although its political power has not been altered, and the measures of effectiveness of state power become limited.

The above description of the socialist version of legitimacy crises reveals the nature of the socialist state and its relationship to civil society. The supremacy of the political system over the economic one is a crucial determinant of production relations (Nove 1982, 601). Control over the property rights, monopolization of the supply of jobs and centralization of planning and management become economic instruments of the state's social policies. The socialist state is no exception to each state's attempt to strengthen and consolidate its power. Under socialism this strengthening of power occurs through economic policy.

The use of the economy for political purposes has several negative aspects, however. First of all, any conflict within the realm of the economy involves the political authorities who sponsor and control the economy. As Galeski has written:

> The centralized system is marked by cumulation of conflicts and a specific unidirectionality of that cumulation. Since the whole society is controlled by the main center of power which monopolizes the administration of all spheres of life, this automatically disrupts self-regulatory mechanisms and relations between the various social classes and groups cannot materialize directly, but must be referred to the main center of power.
> (Galeski 1981, 66)

Since political power does not allow these interests to be institutionalized, a greater politicization of social life results. Second, the centralization and bureaucratization of planning and management become a constraint in the operation of the socialist system and in its economy in particular (see Staniszkis 1979a; 1980). The state's power is undermined by decreased economic efficiency and its inability to plan economic development. Third, the dualism of economic policy, as an instrument of economic development and strengthened political power for the state, undermines both functions.

Economic reforms implemented by the state become the cure for problems caused by the use of the economy for political purposes. Since the state promotes reforms to alleviate the problems created by itself, however, it neglects the interdependence between "economic decentralization and political decentralization" (Hohman 1973, 162). Economic decentralization, as a measure of improving efficiency, potentially endangers political power by loosening the state's control over its sole source of legitimacy--the economy. This is why the state can neither survive without economic reform nor successfully carry it out.

Under these circumstances civil society comes to an understanding of its role as an exclusive social force capable of controlling the socialist state and stimulating the development of the whole political and economic system.

Concluding Remarks

Processes of social development until now have been perceived as subject to political selectivity. From this perspective the state was seen as promoting social change and setting limits to the solutions sought by society. The state was also seen as capable of minimizing opposition to its programs. Recently, however, civil society and/or certain social groups have consciously undertaken the effort to reverse this situation. By refusing to be the object of political decisions, those new collective actors seek the "control of historicity" (Touraine 1982, 77). The struggle by social movements to free societies from state domination has so far been won at least within the cultural sphere (Watts 1983, 55). Social movements stressed the recognition of democracy as a value and emphasized that participation in decision-making processes is crucial for societal survival. The search for has democracy become a universal ideal in both capitalist and socialist societies. In any case, the state is no longer able to solve social problems or to mediate the interests of various social groups.

In the socialist state, however, the exercise of political rights and civil freedoms is but an empty ritual. Formal representative institutions perform symbolic functions only; civil society remains deprived of political rights. In this context Solidarity has not only been the worker's movement, but has also effectively organized, articulated, and transmitted the interests of civil society.

In the capitalist state, the centralized, bureaucratic structure of formal democracy is no longer able to mobilize the society, thus losing considerable popular support and participation. The separation of "mass integrative apparatuses from their social bases" has also excluded the interests of various groups from the political system (Hirsch 1983, 84). Such excluded groups may become the social basis for new movements (Hirsch 1983; Offe 1984; Kesselman 1983) that exceed the scope of labor organizations. Splits within the workforce and the centrality of organized labor have recently diminished. Therefore, social conflicts which arise "from the role of citizenship-citizens as both politically active beings and recipients and consumers of state services" are crucial for this new situation (Offe 1984, 175).

The similarity between new social movements in the West and Solidarity lies in their appeal to citizens and in their goals. In both cases these movements are capable of imposing some degree of self-limitation (Staniszkis 1982, 1984). Under socialism, however, the issue of self-management gains significantly more meaning. Because of the state monopoly over the means of production and means of administration, the predemocratization of the system has to include the implementation of certain self-management measures.

The absence of adequate strategies for democratization and the lack of consensus about participatory democracy remain constant problems for such movements. Despite those shortcomings their role should not be underestimated.

Social movements hold the possibility to effectively implementing social change and forcing the restructuring of the state. Their success depends on the learning capabilities of the system. Socialism, has limited capacity to learn through crises and exhibits a tendency toward ultrastability (Staniszkis 1979b). Capitalism, by contrast, is more flexible and has, as some believe, the ability to learn. There are, however, some macro-limitations of these abilities; for while the capitalist state is restricted by its involvement in the accumulation process, the socialist state is restricted by Soviet doctrine and political practice.

REFERENCES

Arato, Andrew and Jeffrey Goldfarb. 1983. "Introduction." Social Research (Winter).
Galeski, Boguslaw. 1982. "Social Structure--conflicts of Interests--Social Forces in Poland." Sisyphus 3.Warsaw: Polish Scientific Publishers.
Habermas, Jurgen. 1973. Legitimation Crisis. Boston: Beacon Press.
―――――. 1976. Communication and the Evolution of Society. Boston: Beacon Press.
Held, David and Joel Krieger. 1983. "Accumulation, Legitimation and the State: The Ideas of Claus Offe and Jurgen Habermas." David Held et al., eds. States and Societies. Oxford: Martin Robertson.
Hirszowicz, Maria. 1980. The Bureaucratic Leviathan: A Study in the Sociology of Communism. Oxford: Martin Robertson.
Hohman, Hans-Herman. 1979. "The State and the Economy in Eastern Europe." J. Hayward and R. N. Berki, eds. State and Society in Contemporary Europe. Oxford: Martin Robertson.
Jasinska, Alexandra. 1983. "Rationalization and Legitimation Crisis: The Relevance of Marxian and Weberian Works for an Explanation of the Political Order's Legitimacy Crisis in Poland." Sociology 17, no. 2 (May).
Kesselman, Mark. 1983. "From State Theory to Class Struggle and Compromise: Contemporary Marxist Political Studies." Social Science Quarterly, 64, no. 4 (December).
Morawski, Witold. 1982. "The Peculiarities of the Polish Revolution: The System of Articulation of Interests as a Condition of Social Equilibrium." Sisyphus 3.Warsaw: Polish Scientific Publishers.
Nove, Alec. 1982. "Is There a Ruling Class in the USSR?" Anthony Giddens and David Held, eds. Class, Power and Conflict: Classical and Contemporary Debates. Berkeley: University of California Press.
Offe, Claus. 1974. "Structural Problems of the Capitalist State." German Political Studies 1.
―――――. 1983-84. "The Welfare State and the Future of Socialism: An Interview with Claus Offe." Telos 58 (Winter).
Pankow, Wlodzimierz. 1982. "The Roots of the Polish Summer: A Crisis of the System of Power." Sisyphus 3.Warsaw: Polish Scientific Publishers.
Pontusson, Jonas. 1984. "Behind and Beyond New Left Democracy in Sweden." New Left Review 143.

Staniszkis, Jadwiga. 1979a. "Adaptational Super-Structure--The Problem of Negative Self-Regulation." Jerzy Wiatr, ed. Polish Essays in the Methodology of the Social Sciences. Dodrecht and Boston: D. Reidel.
———. 1979b. "On Some Contradictions of Socialist Society: The Case of Poland." Soviet Studies 3.
———. 1982. "Self-Limiting Revolution (One Year Later)." Sisyphus 3. Warsaw: Polish Scientific Publishers.
Strenberger, David. 1968. "Legitimacy." David Sills, ed. International Encyclopedia of Social Sciences. New York: Macmillian.
Watt, Jerry. 1983. "The Socialist as Ostrich: The Unwillingness of the Left to Confront Modernity." Social Research (Spring).

8
Resource Mobilization and Solidarity: Comparing Social Movements across Regimes

Elisabeth Crighton

Whatever Solidarity's future--the advent of martial law ended its legal existence late in 1981--the study of this remarkable enterprise can contribute significantly to scholarship on comparative social movements. One of the many questions worth pursuing is whether similar challenges to the legitimacy of the state might arise in the industrialized nations beyond Poland's borders. This paper addresses that question by comparing certain of Solidarity's goals and attributes to those of social movements in Western Europe and the United States.

Given the significant social, economic, and political differences between Poland and Western nations, our focus on Solidarity may seem arbitrary. Since comparativists usually segregate studies of Eastern and Western Europe, the few attempts to place Solidarity in such a context have usually compared it to other popular opposition movements in Marxist systems (Touraine 1983, 59-63; Paul and Simon 1981; Connor 1980). But there are good, if not obvious, reasons for extending the comparison across regimes. Liberal polities in the West permit numerous and varied forms of popular mobilization and thus can serve as a rich source of hypotheses about collective behavior. More importantly, the literature on comparative social movements abounds in generalizations about all industrial systems, but draws primarily on Western cases. No one has attempted to amend the generalizations with material drawn from social movements under state socialism. This paper can only begin to explore the possibilities for such an expansion of the literature on collective behavior. It does so by applying hypotheses from resource mobilization theory, which rests on a Western (mainly American) empirical base, to account for Solidarity's extraordinary capacity to mobilize more than ten million Poles. It also deduces from the theory five working hypotheses that compare opportunities for mobilization and alliance building in liberal and state socialist polities. The concluding

113

section discusses the attributes of government under state socialism that may leave social movements in those regimes especially vulnerable to failure.

Solidarity as a Total Social Movement

Collective action takes many forms in modern societies, but we take as our subject only those collectivities which, like Solidarity, "act with some continuity to promote or resist a change in the society or group of which [they are] a part" (Turner and Killian 1972, 246). Excluded from this analysis are interest groups (since they do not give priority to social change) and protests (since they organize only episodically). We also exclude, social movements directed toward personal change such as religious sects, cults, or communes. Our interest centers, rather, on movements that organize in order to effect institutional change.

Of these, three types share center stage in the West. The first type, which we may denote as "distributional," includes trade unions, "poor people's movements," and the middle-class coalitions promoting tax reform in Denmark and several American states. Although American trade unions may now be so domesticated as to function more as interest groups than as agencies of social change, unions in Western Europe share with other distributional movements a commitment to promote their class interest. This they do largely by advocating the principles of distributive justice and political inclusion for their members.

"Ethnic nationalist movements," by contrast, have quite a different agenda. These movements reemerged after 1970 in Spain, Belgium, and the Celtic regions of Great Britain, to mention only the most notable cases. Reacting to what they interpret as excessive intrusion into local affairs by centralized and bureaucratic national governments, ethnic nationalists give economic issues a low priority relative to "spiritual" concerns, such as preserving their culture (identity) and acquiring a measure of local self-determination. In fact, leaders of ethnic movements often agitate for regional political autonomy, even when that might prove uneconomical. While distributional movements are rooted in issues of inequality associated with industrialization, ethnic movements appear to speak mainly to problems associated with postindustrialism, especially to the risks to society posed by an overdeveloped "political sector" (Nagel and Olzak 1982, 133).

In this, their interests overlap those of the "new social movements," which have proliferated since the early 1960s. Widely considered to reflect the "postmaterialist" or "postbourgeois" values of an affluent (postindustrial) era, these movements are nonetheless quite diverse. They include national variants of the ecology, women's rights, anti-abortion, peace, antinuclear, and even student movements. What all of the new movements share is a strong, antibureaucratic bias and a preference for decentralized forms of organization, as well as for participatory democracy (Nelkin and Pollack 1981, 1-7; Arato and Cohen 1982; Cohen 1983). By contrast to distributional and ethnic groups, these new political actors also raise moral objections to the impact of technology, the state, and the economy on traditional values (Nelkin and Pollack 1981, 2.).

Given the goal differentiation among social movements in the West, what is interesting about Solidarity is that it combined the central features of all of them: it deals with issues of class, nation (culture) and democracy. Solidarity was, in other words, a "total social movement" because it aimed to change "all aspects of public life" (Touraine 1983, 40-58). In the list of twenty-one demands issued at Gdansk during the strikes of August 1980, Solidarity's Interfactory Strike Committee (MKS) took a strong position on distributional and class concerns. First on the list was a demand for independent unions for workers and at least half the remaining items sought concessions on wages and benefits. From the beginning, Solidarity emphasized its identity as a trade union movement, open only to those employed in Poland's factories and firms.

But to these class-oriented objectives, Solidarity added demands for the institution of guaranteed democratic rights: freedom of the press and publication, freedom of speech, and the right to strike. Item number twelve on the list sounded the antibureaucratic theme of new movements in the West by calling for the selection of management personnel on the strength of their qualifications rather than their membership in the Communist party (PUWP). At a later date, Solidarity also proposed a system of self-management in the workplace, giving to workers the right to name factory directors and to parliament the power to scrutinize state investment and planning decisions.

If Solidarity's goals were expressly distributional and democratic, its spirit and many of its symbols were nationalistic. As new coalitions in the West have been challenging the penetration of society by an overreaching but indigenous state, so Solidarity attempted to rescue Poland's society and economy from a more alien form of domination: the apparatus of the PUWP. It viewed the party not only as incompetent but also as imbued with the "foreign" values of Marxism, which were closer to the Soviet Union's cultural roots than to Poland's own Western heritage. As Michnik put it, Poland had fallen victim to "communism with worn out teeth" (1982, 174). Hence, the symbols associated with the country's new social movement: the cross, a fixture on Lech Walesa's coat lapel and on a wall in Solidarity's Gdansk headquarters; the logo, Solidarnosc, (a Polish flag waving over the letter "n"); and Walesa's moustache, modeled after the one worn by Poland's victor over the Russians in 1920, Marshal Pilsudski (Steven 1982, 175-93).

Certainly, in the breadth of its commitment to social, economic, and political change, Solidarity stands as unique by current Western experience. Only the bourgeois revolutions during the seventeenth century and the mobilization of industrial workers over the last century qualify as analogues (Eder 1982, 10). But this breadth is not all that distinguishes Solidarity from social movements in Western Europe and America. Two other qualities--its size (mobilization ability) and its capacity to build alliances--also mark it as exceptional.

Compared with the reality of social movements elsewhere, the level of mobilization accomplished in Poland within a very short time must be considered extraordinary. At the peak of its strength, Solidarity had organized about 70 percent of the 14 million workers living in the country (Lewis 1982, 144). Just one week after strikers first occupied the Lenin shipyard in Gdansk, strike commitees had formed in 370 enterprises and represented 400,000 strikers (Staniszkis 1981, 209). Mobilization continued even when the Military Council for National Salvation (WRON) imposed martial law. Eventually, one-third of the membership of the PUWP joined, and if we also count ancillary organizations (such as Students Solidarity Committee and Rural Solidarity), it becomes nearly accurate to say that Solidarity "reached into every corner of society" (Steven 1982, 182.

By contrast, consider the record of trade unions in Western Europe. Although unions in Scandinavia, Belgium, and Denmark have organized about 70 percent of the work force, the average level of mobilization in Europe is 40 to 50 percent (in Ireland, Italy, and the United Kingdom). In North America fewer than 30 percent of eligible workers hold union cards (Barkin 1975, 373). Among the newer American movements, civil rights and women's groups have each attracted only 37 percent of their potential supporters (Lewis 1982, 144; Meehan and Bean 1981, 170; Carden 1978, 180). The largest of the European movements, anti-nuclear and environmental groups in West Germany, have pulled in only two million adherents (Nelkin and Pollack 1981, 119-33). At its peak, during the "participation revolution" of 1967-1974, involvement in nonelectoral activity of all kinds reached only 15 to 20 percent of the adult populaton in the United States (Jenkins 1983, 534).

Not only have the citizens in Western nations proven difficult to mobilize, but the theoretical literature from Western sources also holds that participation in organized groups should be low. According to Olson's "logic of collective action" (1965), individuals have no incentive to pursue collective goals by joining organized groups (unless they are coerced or seduced by "selective incentives"), since as "free riders" they will enjoy collective benefits anyhow (for counterarguments, see Kerbo 1982, 652; Jenkins 1983, 536). Other theories of participation hold that those most difficult to mobilize will be persons with fewer resources to devote to political activity (Kerbo 1982, 652). We can deduce from this that social movements should be smaller, not larger, in Poland than is generally true in the affluent countries of the West.

Just as Solidarity mobilized the Poles at a level beyond expectation, it also surpassed the capacity of recent Western movements to attract allies across social classes, occupational groups, and the rural-urban divide. A coalition so broadly based and yet led by working-class leaders (albeit advised by intellectuals) would be unthinkable in most liberal democracies. Political conflict between working-class representatives and Catholic activists is a European tradition, especially in the South, where anticlericalism has fractured trade unions into socialist and Christian-democratic confederations. West European farmers and peasants have never sought alliances with workers, preferring instead to support defensive protests that often run counter to the interests of urban dwellers. Even the student activists of the 1960s could never attract the support they hoped for among members of the working class. How could Solidarity mobilize such a "diversity of social strata and groups" within the relatively restricted political environment of Poland under Gierek (Lewis 1982, 143)?

The Resource Mobilization Perspective

Many accounts, scholarly as well as popular, explain Solidarity's genesis principally as a response to "the Polish crisis," by now well-reported in the Western press. Central to these accounts, although sometimes unexpressed, is the assumption that economic disaster and political crisis produced a widespread sense of grievance against the regime (Bialer 1981; Shapiro 1981; Lewis 1982; Mason 1983). Gierek's unsuccessful strategy for economic development had lowered living standards for many Poles, who were well aware of the incompetence and corruption within Poland's barely legitimate party apparatus. Eventually, the accumulated frustration erupted in a series of strikes, followed by a massive mobilization of

industrial workers. In the vocabulary of traditional sociological theory, Solidarity was a product of "relative deprivation."
   Recent writings on social movements argue for a more elaborate causal model than the traditional theories of collective behavior have so far developed. Without denying the force of psychological predispositions to collective action, the new research (referred to as the "resource mobilization perspective"), treats social movements as outcomes tied to a confluence of factors. These include social and political structure (Skocpol 1979) social movement organization and access to resources (McCarthy and Zald 1973, 1977; Law and Walsh 1983) or some combination of all of these (Tilly 1978; Oberschall 1973; Kerbo 1982; Jenkins 1983).
   In the analysis that follows, we will draw on propositions from resource mobilization theory to illuminate the resource costs and benefits, as well as the political relationships, involved in Solidarity's mobilization as a total social movement. We will attempt to establish relationships between two independent variables (Solidarity's access to resources and organizational structure) and two dependent variables (its capacity to mobilize and to build alliances.).

Resources and Social Mobilization

   If one defines mobilization as a social movement's capacity to attract adherents, then Solidarity was very highly mobilized indeed. But a more restricted usage requires mobilizers to demonstrate "control over resources they previously did not control" (Tilly 1978, 69). Even by this standard, Solidarity's attainments are impressive. The movement acquired a clear collective identity, which extended well beyond its home borders, and a collection of associated symbols and slogans. At a more advanced level of control, it operated through a system of organization centered on the MKS, whose presidium had authority to speak for Solidarity as a whole on national matters. During the Gdansk strike, the presidium controlled practically the entire region of Gdansk-Gdynia: on a given day, it decided which sections of the local public transport system would be open, directed food shipments to local stores, and coordinated internal security, food supplies, and information for the striking workers (Staniszkis 1981, 210).
   After its registration, NSZZ Solidarnosc (the Independent, Self-Governing Trade Union, Solidarity) acquired its own territory. It had a national headquarters in Gdansk, local bureaus in many Polish cities and towns, and offices within many enterprises. Its directorate (National Commission) could pay a number of cadres and rely on a much larger contingent of 40,000

unpaid organizers. Solidarity, in other words, had taken on the qualities of a "complex organization."
There is evidence that Solidarity also maintained a substantial though far from perfect degree of organizational self-discipline. Shapiro has described the usual pattern of industrial action in Poland as one of "price increases generating walkouts which rapidly degenerate into uncontrolled street rioting, culminating in the burning down of a local party office, confrontation with police, and a belligerent return to work all within the space of a few days..." (1981, 494). But in 1980 the workers organized very quickly, by establishing factory strike committees. Good organization at the grass roots resulted in a nonviolent, tightly organized, and well-coordinated series of strikes that could be escalated as necessary to support Solidarity's negotiating position. The result was "the longest and most widespread industrial outburst in postwar Polish history" (Shapiro 1981, 494-95). Although internal unity declined in later months, as Solidarity attempted to institutionalize its legal position, the movement never ceased to operate as labor's coordinator and chief negotiator in bargaining with the Kania regime.
Resource mobilization theory holds that a social movement's capacity to mobilize support and establish organizational self-discipline correlates with its access to resources, specifically, "the greater the absolute amount of resources available, the greater the likelihood that new social movements will develop" (McCarthy and Zald 1977, 1225). Much has been written about the nature of these resources, but in this paper we need distinguish only between their tangible and intangible forms (Jenkins 1983, 533). The former includes money, facilities, and means of communication; the latter, such "human assets" as legal expertise, organizational ability, and social bonds based on loyalty or obligation (Tilly 1978, 69).
In terms only of its access to tangible resources, mobilization theory suggests that Solidarity should never have taken off. Zald has argued that high levels of social control, or repression, will dampen collective activity, presumably by blocking access to resources for social movements. Even in open polities, social movements that confront centralized political institutions will have fewer opportunities to make their claims (Zald 1980, 69). We can deduce, then, the following:

Hypothesis 1: State socialist regimes raise the cost of entry to social movements by restricting their access to money, means of communication, and other tangible resources.

In Poland, as elsewhere in Eastern Europe, such restrictions have been well documented. Even after the Gdansk agreement had established its right to exist and to strike, Solidarity struggled to acquire assets. Polish law did not permit the new union to transfer funds from the official unions it had replaced, nor did the law permit independent unions beyond the Baltic region (Staniszkis 1981, 219). Although ultimately, the Kania government did reach a national agreement with Solidarity, it consistently broke or put off implementing most of the twenty-one points of the Gdansk accord.

It would be wrong, however, to conclude that Solidarity lacked tangible resources altogether. Years of rapid economic growth between 1945 and the late 1950s had increased Poland's standard of living. Another high-growth period between 1970 and 1975 pushed average incomes up some 40 percent, greatly improving supplies of food and consumer durables. Housing and transport facilities benefited as well (Woodall 1981, 38; Lewis 1982, 140; Shapiro 1981, 471). Shortages, which resulted after 1975 from Gierek's failed "dash for growth," did indeed leave many Poles feeling aggrieved, but earlier economic advances may well have improved their capacity to take political action.

Poland also operated under a "comparatively benign system of Communist control," characterized by restrained use of the secret police and other tools of social control (Steven 1982, 4; Kay 1979, 8). As a consequence, the penetration of Polish society by the state was less extensive than elsewhere in Eastern Europe and the autonomy of potential opposition groups that much greater. After the food riots of 1976, some of these groups set up a communications network of underground publications in order to broadcast information about the regime's treatment of its critics, especially workers and intellectuals. The network would later serve as the core around which Solidarity's own information service could be built (Woodall 1981, 54; Paul and Simon 1981, 26, 32).

It was, however, in the realm of intangible resources that Solidarity's substantial assets lay. Although some observers thought the movement had emerged "overnight," in truth, significant if relatively uncoordinated mobilization had begun at least four years before the Gdansk strikes of July and August 1980. This "societal infrastructure" of support for Solidarity consisted of two elements: the Polish Catholic Church along with its lay organizations and a loose network of secular groups and clubs (for detailed analysis see chapters 4 and 5 of this volume).

That Solidarity should have benefited from such a "societal infrastructure of support" confirms one of the central hypotheses of resource mobilization theory:

that intangible resources can compensate incipient social movements for their restricted access to tangible assets. The theory also holds that under some conditions an infrastructure of support may help overcome "free rider" disincentives to collective action by encouraging movements to recruit en bloc from existing solidary groups (Jenkins 1983, 537). Oberschall argues that "bloc recruitment" is the most efficient form of mobilization and appears to be typical of large-scale movements for institutional change (1973, 125). This is so for two reasons. First, new movements can reduce their resource costs of organizing by building on existing group structures (Tilly 1978, 81). Second, "natural groups" with "distinctive identities" and "dense interperson networks" can offer "normative assets" (natural loyalties and obligations), which serve as solidary incentives for collective action (Jenkins 1983, 538). Tilly hypothesizes that the more highly organized these natural groups, the more readily accessible to mobilization they will be (1978, 62-63). Political scientists have drawn a parallel conclusion from their studies of political participation, finding that participation varies directly with levels of organizational membership across the industrialized democracies (La Palombara 1974, 456). Even in those cases in which social movements apparently arise from nowhere in response to a catalyzing crisis or event, resource mobilization theory holds that their formation "presupposes the existence of resourceful, organized groups" (McCarthy and Zald 1977 in Turner 1981, 16).

The recent pattern of mobilization in Poland suggests that the intangible resources helpful to the formation of social movements are thus not limited to Western liberal democracies. We certainly cannot preclude the possibility of collective action against other states in Eastern Europe, since even the most repressive policies are not guaranteed to destroy those natural groups that feed collective action. Such a level of social control requires a substantial penetration by the state into society; any survey of Eastern Europe will confirm that state socialist regimes vary in this capacity. We can therefore deduce from resource mobilization theory that socialist regimes may restrict access to tangible resources, but they cannot so successfully deny intangible resources to prospective social movements. Therefore:

<u>Hypothesis 2</u>: The stronger the infrastructure of support, the lower the costs of entry and the more likely the formation of social movements under state socialism.

Organization, Resource Competition, and Alliance-Building

We now turn to the sources of Solidarity's capacity to consolidate diverse forces in Polish society. Solidarity did more than pull workers, farmers, and intellectuals into a massive trade union movement. It also united these groups in a cooperative enterprise unprecedented in modern Polish experience. Scholarly explanations for this usually turn on three characteristics of Polish culture and society: the coincidence of an integrated social structure, a history of national unity, and a level of moral consensus rarely found in industrialized settings.

Poland's social structure derives largely from its late industrialization. Before 1940, 60 percent of the population lived on the land (Steven 1982, 199), which means of course that a substantial proportion of Poland's present working population comes from peasant stock. Familial ties between manual workers, farmers, and the intelligentsia are stronger than those among working people in the more fully industrialized countries elsewhere in Europe. Woodall argues that low social mobility since 1975 has also blurred the boundary between manual and white collar jobs, since highly trained job seekers, who would have been managers in more prosperous times, must now accept lower positions (for example, the post of factory foreman) that bring them into contact with manual workers (1981, 45-48). It would, of course, be a mistake to ignore the important social differentiation that has taken place in Poland since the end of World War II (Paul and Simon 1981, 30). But it is still accurate to characterize the country's social structure as relatively well-integrated by the standards of other industrialized societies.

This, perhaps, explains why Poles today show a high level of agreement on social and political values, embracing such principles as equality of opportunity, freedom of speech, and freedom to practice a religion. Surveys have turned up no evidence of a generational or urban-rural attitude cleavage (Paul and Simon 1981, 33-34). Successful efforts to maintain national unity, even during long periods of statelessness, have reinforced this consensus by enhancing the symbolic importance of the Catholic Church and, therefore, its influence on popular opinion.

These sociocultural attributes undoubtedly enhanced Solidarity's capacity to build alliances among the diverse groups of Polish society. In the terminology of resource mobilization theory, they served as "normative resources" for mobilization. But they tell us little of Solidarity's own role in converting a spontaneous shipyard sit-in into a complex organization of ten million members. Neither do they explain how Solidarity managed to consolidate Poland's loose network of oppositional groups, when the mobilizations of 1968, 1970, and 1976 had not. Presumably, the same sociocultural conditions operated in all of these cases.

Although resource mobilization theorists acknowledge the sociocultural setting's influence on collective behavior, they give other variables pride of place as correlates of cooperation (alliance-building) within social movements. For Zald and McCarthy (1980), these are organization and resource competition. Adopting for a moment their economistic language, we can describe social movements as "congeries" of particular "social movement organizations" (SMOs). Those pursuing similar goals belong to a "social movement industry," characterized by competition for scarce resources. Social movements (or social movement industries) thus include two kinds of structures: their constituent SMOs and the relationships among SMOs (see also McCarthy and Zald 1973, 1977). Described in these terms, Solidarity may be considered a social movement industry comprised of numerous SMOs: the free trade unions (federated as NSZZ Solidarnosc), Rural Solidarity, Students Solidarity Committee, KOR, and many others. What we wish to explain in this section is why Solidarity became a movement of "consolidated pluralism," characterized by cooperation among its SMOs, rather than a replica of the model of "competitive pluralism" associated with the Czech mobilization of 1968 and Western social movements of the present (Paul and Simon 1981, 34-36).

Mobilization theory holds that cooperative relations among SMOs in the same industry increase as follows: functional differentiation or task specialization increases, permitting each movement organization to carve out its special function and then engage in cooperative exchange with similarly specialized organizations (Zald and McCarthy 1980, 11); overlapping constituencies or multiple memberships reduce the social exclusiveness of any one SMO (Zald and McCarthy 1980, 5, 13); and interlocking directorates and overlapping leadership reduce the level of segmentation among leaders of potentially competitive SMOs (Zald and McCarthy 1980, 12).

The very nature of the organizational explosion antecedent to Solidarity assured a certain task specialization, as its constituent SMOs took on functions appropriate to the occupational groups from which they recruited. Intellectuals specialized in informational and planning tasks (for example, documentation, research, and communication), while workers assumed the burden of direct action to protest official economic policies. Farmers, students, and professionals all specialized in concerns particular to their places in the social structure, avoiding competition for supporters because they did not organize across occupational boundaries.

What evolved after 1976, however, was a tendency by these functional groups to support the industrial workers as agents of direct action. In 1976 a group of intellectuals sent a letter to the Seym, protesting the government's treatment of the workers who had rioted in June. KOR began advising cells of workers on organizational tactics and goals for further industrial action (Steven 1982, 234). Thereafter, it published in its newspaper, Robotnik, an "action program" for workers and a "charter of workers' rights" (Kay 1979, 11). KOR also established its own Legal Intervention Bureau to uncover repressive acts by the authorities and, where possible, to mediate. Its Social Self-Defense Fund provided financial aid for those whose political activities had cost them their jobs or put them in legal jeopardy (Drawicz 1979, 36). KOR built new alliances among workers, students, and intellectuals through its "Flying University," founded by sixty-two Polish scholars in 1978 to teach "alternative courses" outside the university curriculum. By 1979, courses were being held in homes and churches in every university town in Poland (Steven 1982, 234).

Since intellectuals had already established relationships with workers in the wake of the 1976 riots, they could quite naturally rally to Solidarity after the Gdansk strikes broke out in August 1980. Soon afterward, 260 intellectuals sent a petition of support for Solidarity to the Central Committee of the PUWP. The Polish Political Science and Sociological Associations circulated letters exhorting the government to negotiate with the MKS. Once the government had agreed to negotiate, intellectuals from KOR served as experts attached to Solidarity's presidium.

Support from SMOs representing other occupational groups and interests also emerged. On July 20, the Committee of the Farmers Independent Trade Unions and several rural self-defense committees sent Solidarity a letter of support (Shapiro 1981, 496). Representatives of the Young Poland Movement, strongly anti-Russian and antiregime, camped in the Lenin Shipyard with the strikers throughout Walesa's negotiations with the government. Also in the Lenin Shipyard during this period were delegates of the discussion club Experience and Future (DIP), some of whose adherents were members of the PUWP. The Catholic Church gave its early, but guarded, support for the demands of the strikers.

Overlapping memberships also facilitated cooperation between the free trade unions and other SMOs. Solidarity included many members of KOR in the ranks of its expert advisers (some would later blame the experts for unduly tempering the movement's objectives). Rural Solidarity brought farmers into the trade union movement. Although they could not join Solidarity by right of occupation, some doctors and lawyers continued to work on its behalf. The movement even reached into the ranks of the Communist party: radical, antibureaucratic rump groups within many local units of the PUWP contributed over 700,000 members to Solidarity (Staniszkis 1979, 211). One third of the MKS belonged to the party.

But resource mobilization theory suggests that other pressures toward cooperation among Solidarity's constituent SMOs may also have been at work within Polish society, indeed, that these may operate within state socialist regimes in general. Zald and McCarthy (1980, 11) have hypothesized that social control or repression threatens the existence of a number of social movement organizations will encourage them to cooperate in their own defense (See also Tilly 1978, 100-14). "Clear cut and vigorous countermovements" will also lead to defensive alliances among SMOs (1980, 16). Functioning somewhat ineffectually as a countermovement, the PUWP attempted to eviscerate Solidarity by various means, as both the press and the scholarly literature have reported (Steven 1982; Weschler 1983). Shapiro has concluded that a reactive "logic of escalation" worked to expand the movement, since "individual participants might feel less vulnerable to subsequent reprisal as the lines of confrontation expanded numerically and geographically" (1981, 495). As there is every reason to suppose that political elites in other state socialist systems will behave in a similar manner toward oppositional movements, we can deduce from resource mobilization theory:

Hypothesis 3: The more intense the countermobilization and the greater the use of repression by political elites, the stronger the incentives for cooperation among SMOs under state socialism.

Another factor that may also encourage these organizations to cooperate involves what theorists refer to as "product differentiation." Western cases have suggested that social movement organizations sharing the same goal will compete for support by differentiating themselves according to tactics or strategy. The greater the opportunity for such "product differentiation," the greater their competition for resources (Zald and McCarthy 1980, 6). Several characteristics of state socialism make it logical to assume that opportunities for product differentiation will be limited in East European polities. Political centralization offers fewer avenues of access to authority and therefore fewer strategic choices than do systems in which power is more widely dispersed. Limitations on resource availability should also reduce opportunities for product differentiation. Governmental countermobilization and the use of repression should further limit the tactical and strategic options available to social movements. We can thus deduce the following:

> Hypothesis 4: The fewer the opportunities for product differentiation, the less intense the competition for scarce resources and the greater the cooperation among SMOs under state socialism.

If these deductions are correct--and it is important to note that they await further empirical tests--then we can deduce from resource mobilization theory a final hypothesis about the behavior of social movements under state socialism. McCarthy and Zald have found in Western polities that product differentiation within competitive social movement industries encourages SMOs to "offer narrow goals and strategies" (1977, 1234). Insofar as movements in socialist systems face pressures for cooperation rather than competition, we should expect their goals to be commensurately broad. Thus, we can deduce:

> Hypothesis 5: The lower the resource competition, the greater the cooperation among SMO's under state socialism and the broader their goals and strategies.

The logic of the foregoing implies that "Solidarity-type" total social movements could well evolve across the board in Eastern Europe. Such a conclusion is, however, premature. Restrictions on resource availability do inhibit collective action in authoritarian regimes. Moreover, the variables we have identified using resource mobilization theory may exclude others relevant to the course of collective action. Even if that were not the case, we would need to attach weights to each variable and learn something of their causal sequence before attempting to predict the course of oppositional activity in state socialist regimes. Quite possibly, Solidarity's progress has been overdetermined, the consequence of a confluence of circumstances particular to the present period of Polish history. If this is so, it will be difficult to reproduce a similar social movement in another setting. Thus, the conclusions drawn so far must be treated cautiously.

Conclusion

Resource mobilization theory has directed us to consider variables other than relative deprivation or the existence of grievances for an explanation of Solidarity's size and breadth. Additional correlates, this paper argues, are the movement's access to resources and its organizational structure. It is also possible that the nature of state socialism as a political regime may help account for Solidarity's capacity to consolidate Poland's oppositional groups. The use of repression by party elites and inherent restrictions on product differentiation may have encouraged such groups to cooperate in their own defense. These pressures toward cooperation in turn could help account for the breadth of Solidarity's goals.

We have also concluded that total social movements on the model of Solidarity may occur more readily under state socialism than in the competitive social movement industries of liberal democratic regimes. Political regimes, in other words, may be more than incidental in the formation of social movements. While state socialist systems can erect high barriers to entry, restricting the number of movements that form by limiting access to resources, mobilization theory leads to the conclusion that those that do take hold will be larger, more inclusive, and have broader goals than their counterparts in the more "open" political arenas of the West.

This is not to say, however, that total social movements will emerge often in the regimes of Eastern Europe. Since they drive from a confluence of factors, it is more reasonable to suppose that such movements will occur rarely indeed. Even taking into account the pressures for cooperation among SMOs under state socialism, one can argue that other ingredients necessary to total movements may be missing in many Eastern polities. Such a movement as Solidarity would appear improbable in Czechoslovakia, where regional and ethnic divisions have created an environment of "competitive pluralism" and in 1968 spawned a social movement far less solidary than Poland's. In Hungary we note the absence of a strong infrastructure of support for opposition and a Catholic Church much less influential than the Polish church. Beyond these Central European countries, with their history of exposure to democratic values, there is even less reason to expect the growth of a large oppositional movement.

Thus far we have put aside the important problem of explaining why some social movements are better able than others to "realize a program for the reform of society" (Turner and Killian 1972, 256): that is, to be successful. Resource mobilization theory does not address this question systematically. Rather it has focused on understanding how social movements form and take shape (Turner 1981, 9). But we can speculate here on two factors the literature proposes as relevant.

According to Zald and Ash (1966, 327-41), social movements are more likely to realize their goals when these are congruent with their organizational structure. Decentralized SMOs maximize the possibility of attracting a large following at the grass roots and of transforming the values of their participants (Jenkins 1983, 539), but decentralization produces lower strategic effectiveness than bureaucratic organizations can provide. Decentralization also has the advantages of generating new ideas and tactical innovations, as well as complicating official attempts at social control (ibid.). But more centralized and professional SMOs can better coordinate their members; they are also likely to initiate successful programs of institutional change (Zald and Ash 1966, 327-41).

SMOs will run into problems when they attempt to combine all of these organizational features within a single framework to maximize their ability to attract members, generate new ideas, control resources, and win concessions from political elites. Efforts to reach such multiple goals can generate internal tensions, reducing a movement's ultimate effectiveness. Solidarity was, of course, no stranger to intraorganizational tension. Even during the negotiations of August 1980, some of its members objected to what they interpreted as excessive control by Lech Walesa and the presidium he led. After Solidarity's legalization, power conflicts divided members of the National Commission, the regional presidiums, and the local unions. In some cases, these divisions led to wildcat strikes initiated at the factory level (Staniszkis 1979, 226). Periodic demands for a rotation of leadership also surfaced at the grass roots. After martial law had forced the movement underground, some adherents criticized the presidium in Gdansk for failing to restrain radical elements sufficiently to avoid military rule (Steven 1982, 396). A similar tension between the goals of centralization and democratic decentralization may be found in the recent writings of Solidarity's former experts (Kuron 1982; Michnik 1982).

A particular problem for social movements under state socialism is the fact that they must confront highly centralized political institutions whose incumbents will repress or otherwise try to control collective action when it arises. As Staniszkis has described the Polish regime's "mirror effect" on Solidarity, Walesa and others in the leadership tried to counter the movement's inherent tendencies toward disunity in order to deprive the PUWP of opportunities for exploitation (1981, 227). Adam Michnik, a central figure among Solidarity's expert advisers, has captured the essence of this dilemma in his description of the movement as a "colossus with steel feet but clay hands." Movements based on democratic values often have difficulty reconciling these with the instrumental necessity of establishing organizational control, but authoritarian institutions under state socialism may exacerbate such tensions by creating an "organizational imperative" toward centralizaion.

Resource mobilization theory also identifies a second factor important to the success of social movements: the formation of coalitions between their activists and political elites (Skocpol 1979, 11; Tilly 1978, 132-33; Jenkins 1983, 546). This point has not escaped some of those who participated in Solidarity. Staniszkis, a former adviser to the presidium of Gdansk Solidarity, has written that the trade union movement's best chance for success lay in establishing "an alliance with the anti-bureaucratic, younger generation in the party apparatus" (1981, 220). Despite the presence of thousands of party activists within Solidarity's ranks, such a link never materialized. Herein lies another way in which political regimes are important contributors to the success or failure of social movements. Under state socialism, the costs of building coalitions with party elites will be higher than those faced by movements in liberal regimes. The pattern of reciprocal influence and co-optation characteristic of governments and social movements in the West may not so easily obtain in the East, since elites under state socialism are relatively well insulated from the populations they govern.

In the Polish case, where a reasonably durable infrastructure of opposition assures Solidarity's continued (if submerged) existence, one can only foresee a stand-off: a permanent state of disequilibrium between a regime unable to eliminate its opponents and an opposition unable to effect the institutional changes it seeks.

REFERENCES

Arato, Andrew and Jean Cohen. 1982. "The Peace Movement and Western European Sovereignty." Telos 51.

Barkin, Solomon. 1975. Worker Militancy and its Consequences, 1965-75. New York: Praeger.

Bialer, Seweryn. 1981. "Poland and the Soviet Imperium." Foreign Affairs 59.

Carden, Maren. 1978. "The Proliferation of a Social Movement: Ideology and Individual Incentives in the Contemporary Feminist Movement." Louis Kriesberg, ed. Research in Social Movements, Conflicts and Change. 1, Greenwich, Conn.: JAI Press.

Cohen, Jean. 1982. "Between Crisis Management and Social Movements: The Place of Institutional Reforms." Telos 52.

_____. 1983. "Rethinking Social Movements." Berkeley Journal of Sociology 28.

Connor, Walter. 1980. "Dissent in Eastern Europe." Problems of Communism 29.

Denitch, Bogdan. 1982. "Social Movements in The Reagan Era." Telos 53.

Drawicz, Andrzej. 1979. "Experience of Democratic Opposition in Poland." Survey 24, 4 (109).

Dubet, Francois, Alain Touraine and Michel Wiewiorka. 1982. "A Social Movement: Solidarity." Telos 53.

Eder, Klaus. 1982. "A New Social Movement?" Telos 52.

Feher, Ferenc and Agnes Heller. 1982. "The Antinomies of Peace." Telos 53.

Gurney, Joan and Kathleen Tierney. 1982. "Relative Deprivation and Social Movements: A Critical Look at Twenty Years of Theory and Research." The Sociological Quarterly. 23.

Habermas, Jurgen. 1975. Legitimation Crisis. Boston: Beacon Press.

_____. 1981. "New Social Movements." Telos 49.

Holt, Robert and John Turner, eds. 1970. The Methodology of Comparative Research. New York: Free Press.

Jenkins, J. Craig. 1983. "Resource Mobilization Theory and the Study of Social Movements." Annual Review of Sociology 9.

Kay, Joseph. 1979. "The Polish Opposition." Survey 24, No. 4 (109).

Kerbo, Harold. 1982. "Movements of 'Crisis' and Movements of 'Affluence': A Critique of Deprivation and Resource Mobilization Theories." Journal of Conflict Resolution 26, No. 4.

Kolakowski, Leszek. 1979. "Emergence of the Opposition: Introduction." Survey 24, No. 4.

Kuron, Jacek. 1982. "How to Get Out of a Dead-End Situation." Telos 51.
La Palombara, Joseph. 1974. Politics Within Nations. Englewood Cliffs, N.J.: Prentice Hall.
Law, Kim and Edward Walsh. 1983. "The Interaction of Grievances and Structures in Social Movement Analysis: the Case of JUST." The Sociological Quarterly 24.
Lewis, Paul. 1982. "Obstacles to the Establishment of Political Legitimacy in Poland." British Journal of Political Science 12.
McCarthy, John and Mayer Zald. 1973. The Trend of Social Movements. Morristown, N.J.: General Learning.
———. 1977. "Resource Mobilization and Social Movements: A Partial Theory." American Journal of Sociology 82, No. 6.
Mason, David. 1983. "Policy Dilemmas and Political Unrest in Poland." Journal of Politics 45, No. 2.
Meehan, Anita and Glynis Bean. 1981. "Tracking the Civil Rights and Women's Movements in the United States." International Journal of Intercultural Relations 5.
Meluccci, Alberto. 1980. "The New Social Movements: A Theoretical Approach." Social Science Information 19, No. 2.
Michnik, Adam. 1982. "We Are All Hostages." Telos 51.
Nagel, Joane and Susan Olzak. 1982. "Ethnic Mobilization in New and Old States: An Extension of the Competition Model." Social Problems 30, No. 2.
Nelkin, Dorothy and Michal Pollack. 1981. The Atom Besieged: Extraparliamentary Dissent in France and Germany. Cambridge, Mass.: MIT Press.
Oberschall, Anthony. 1973. Social Conflict and Social Movements. Englewood Cliffs, N.J.: Prentice-Hall.
Olson, Mancur. 1965. The Logic of Collective Action. Cambridge, Mass.: Harvard University Press.
Olzak, Susan. 1983. "Contemporary Ethnic Mobilization." Annual Review of Sociology 9.
Paul, David and Maurice Simon. 1981. "Poland Today and Czechoslovakia, 1968." Problems of Communism 30.
Pospieszalski, Antoni. 1979. "Lay Catholic Organizations in Poland." Survey 24, No. 4 (109).
Ramirez, Francisco. 1981. "Comparative Social Movements." International Journal of Comparative Sociology 22, Nos. 1-2.

Shapiro, Ian. 1981. "Fiscal Crisis of the Polish State: Genesis of the 1980 Strikes." Theory and Society 10, No. 4.
Skocpol, Theda. 1979. States and Social Revolutions. New York: Cambridge University Press.
Staniszkis, Jadwiga. 1981. "The Evolution of Forms of Working-Class Protest in Poland: Sociological Reflections on the Gdansk-Szczcin Case, August 1980." Soviet Studies 33, No. 2.
Steven, Stewart. 1982. "The Poles. New York: Macmillan.
Svitak, Ivan. 1982. "Lessons From Poland." Telos 52.
Swidlicki, Andrzej. 1982. "Experience and the Future" and the Polish Crisis." Telos 53.
Szafar, Tadeusz. 1979. "Contemporary Political Opposition In Poland." Survey, 24, No. 4 (109).
Szczypiorski, Andrzej. 1979. "The Limits of Political Realism." Survey 24, No. 4.
Tilly, Charles. 1978. From Mobilization to Revolution. Reading, Mass.: Addison-Wesley.
Touraine, Alain et al. 1983. Solidarity: The Analysis of a Social Movement, Poland 1980-81. New York: Cambridge University Press.
Turner, Ralph. 1981. "Collective Behavior and Resource Mobilization as Approaches to Social Movements: Issues and Continuities." Louis Kriesberg, ed. Research in Social Movements, Conflict and Change. Greenwich, Conn.: JAI Press.
Verba, Sidney, Norman Nie and Jae-On Kim. 1971. The Modes of Democratic Participation: A Cross-National Comparison. Beverly Hills, Ca: Sage Publications.
Weschler, Lawrence. 1983. "A State of War, I and II." New Yorker. April 11 and 18.
Woodall, Jean. 1981. "New Social Factors in the Unrest in Poland." Government and Opposition 16, No. 1.
Zald, Mayer. 1980. "Issues in the Theory of Social Movements." Scott McNall and Gary Howe, eds. Current Perspectives in Social Theory 1, Greenwich, Conn.: JAI Press.
_____ and John McCarthy. 1980. "Social Movement Industries: Competition and Cooperation Among Movement Organizations." Louis Kriesberg, eds. Research in Social Movements, Conflicts and Change 3 Greenwich, Conn.: JAI Press.

9
Beyond Solidarity: Democratic-Symbolic Ruminations
Scott Warren

There has been surprisingly little discussion in the United States about the ongoing experience and implications of the Solidarity movement in Poland. While various journal articles do exist and a few book-length works are now appearing, there is hardly any general public discourse about the phenomenon. The ignorance and everyday disdain of Solidarity is to some extent due to the general crisis of democracy in the United States, to the near-death of serious rational discourse on important public issues, and, of course, to the media-managed limits of our public attention span.

But there is another important reason for our relative lack of interest in the continuing struggles and developments inside Poland. It concerns the fact that there is a crucial perspective missing from our usual analysis and interpetation of the issue, a perspective that might be called "dialectical" or "neo-Marxist". I shall suggest that this perspective allows us to reorient our view of Solidarity's significance and to develop implications of the movement that can contribute to broadening our understanding of democracy and its future. The following ruminations thus deviate from the usual methodological constraints in order to provoke reflection and raise questions at a different level of concern than is usually done when dealing with the dimensions of the Solidarity movement.

Most of the conventional views of Solidarity's meaning and importance, especially in the United States, tend to focus on the general breakdown and failure of socialism as a system. One of the most common views, of course, argues that Solidarity is (or at least began as) a social movement of trade unionism. Its aims were formulated in terms of ameliorating the conditions of certain workers in specific, narrow, and concrete terms. Such a view implies that Solidarity at best revealed the economically backward state of Poland when contrasted with the West, where trade unions exist with some relative measure of power and influence in the state. From this perspective, the success or failure of Solidarity could be measured by its ability to exact concessions, based on a long list of unionlike grievances from the state bureaucracy. Such a view implies that should Solidarity succeed, then socialism might suffer a serious weakening of its monolithic and totalitarian hold on society and begin a slow process of withering away.

Behind the view of Solidarity as primarily a movement of trade unionism lies a more fundamental assumption regarding the general internal weakness, inefficiency, and inevitable failure of socialism as an economic and political way of life. To many observers, the very emergence of Solidarity signals a breakdown of socialism economically and reveals its inability to provide goods and services on a par with "market economies." The failure of a socialist system to pacify its workers reveals a deeper, almost "natural" impulse toward the reemergence of capitalist forms of organization to provide for fair wages, productive efficiency, price stability, and the like. This view takes pleasure in discovering confirmation of the eternal, inherent flaws in socialist modes of production. The reaction of the Polish state to the social disruption caused by Solidarity simply reveals further the politically authoritarian and repressive nature of socialist societies. When confronted with its internal economic collapse, the system thus responds with its natural tendency toward undemocratic, repressive solutions.

These kinds of perspectives are quite attractive within the context of a neo-Cold War atmosphere and attitude. What seems to be at the root of many interpretations of Solidarity's significance is a bipolar view of political dissidence. Perhaps one of the most powerful interpretations of Solidarity is that it represents a large collective form of political dissidence a la Solzhenitsyn—that is, self-conscious collective dissent from the ideals of socialism themselves. This is a particularly prevalent perspective in the context of international relations, where the syllogistic formula often reads as follows: the Soviet Union is the fount and essence of socialism; Solidarity represents a rebellion against the Soviet Union and Poland's rule by the Communist Party; therefore Solidarity represents an attack on the core of socialist ideals and marks a triumph for the ideological, social, economic, and political supremacy of the West. And, therefore, Solidarity becomes simply one more symbolic and real pawn in the global ideological maneuvering game between the United States and the Soviet Union.

Regardless of the relative merits and demerits of these perspectives, which I have only sketched here, it may be the case that the significance of Solidarity is much different and broader than such views would allow. It may be that such perspectives miss some of the more important implications of Solidarity for democratic theory in general. If we adopt a dialectical or neo-Marxist viewpoint, which has no theoretical or ideological stake in either Western or Soviet perceptions of either Solidarity or democracy in general, then we might be freed to speculate on some of the radical democratic implications of the movement. We might find that such speculation points in a direction that is uncomfortable for both American and Soviet models of democratic society.

Before outlining some of the democratic implications that can point us beyond Solidarity, it might help to summarize the essence of a dialectical Marxist perspective and discuss why its distinction from positivist Marxism is so crucial for both theoretical and practical reasons.* Throughout the twentieth century, the predominant development of Marxist theory has been guided by a positivist theory of knowledge and conception of the world. The Marxism of Plekhanov, Bukharin, Lenin, the Second International, Stalin, Suslov, and so on, is underpinned by a view that thought and knowledge are reflections of the "laws" of history and society. If theoretical concepts and understanding simply reflect the lawlike relations of the world, then the relation between theory and practice is construed in such a way as to vitiate much of the emancipatory, humanistic, and democratic content and import of Marxist political theory. In such an interpretation political practice becomes little more than the technical application of the nomological principles discovered through scientific-socialist analysis in an attempt to predict and manipulate social reality.

Such a positivist and technocratic view of knowledge and its relationship to political practice has had no or little impact on the political development of Marxism in our time. Rather than developing as a politics involving communal human action and interaction that is open, self-critical, and liberating, most Marxist political practice (based on a positivist self-interpretation) has moved in a nondialectical direction where the theory-practice relation is construed only in instrumental terms. Rather than finding free, human, laboring praxis emerging as the "metasubject" of history, we find the party playing that role. Resembling an impoverished version of Hegel's

---

*For a more thorough discussion of the crucial distinction between dialectical and positivist Marxism, see my The Emergence of Dialectical Theory: Philosophy and Political Inquiry (Chicago: University of Chicago Press, 1984).

"absolute spirit," the party works upon and molds the social life of citizens as the "matter" of its knowledge and will.

"Dialectical Marxism," which has been developed in our century by such theorists as Gramsci, Lukacs, Horkeimer, Kolakowski, Merleau-Ponty, Marcuse, Habermas, and others, offers a radically different view of knowledge and reality. Knowledge involves the active engagement of consciousness in a reciprocal relation with the world and in such a way as to event the hubris of social engineering. The relation between theory and practice is open-ended and depends on the self-constitution of a free society by the citizens themselves. A dialectical Marxism stands opposed to any deterministic view of history as well as to any economic determinism within society itself.

The distinction between dialectical and positivist Marxism, at which I am only hinting here, is not as abstract and subtle as it might appear. There are enormous political implications and effects of such a distinction. Any Marxist politics guided by a positive view of Marxist theory is inevitably doomed to result in the undemocratic pseudo-fulfillment of socialist ideals. Regardless of the content or substance of such fulfillment, the form it takes is inescapably one of false-consciousness, instrumentalist social engineering, and authoritarian (or bureaucratic) domination. Most Marxist politics has been guided by such a view, while dialectical Marxism is indeed remarkably distinguished by a history of failing to find expression in any effective or enduring political party or practice.

I submit that such a gap between dialectical Marxist theory and positivist Marxist politics does not indicate the theoretical deficiency of a dialectical and critical Marxism, but instead the inordinate difficulty of effecting the liberating union of humanist philosophy and political practice (something Plato understood well). It also points up the dangerous possibility and relative ease of descending into a positivist, technocratic approach to politics (whether Marxist or non-Marxist), compared to ascending to the level of free, nonexploitative human interaction. Social engineering is easier than democracy. The criterion of "it works" is much simpler to grasp than that of "it emancipates." Such a state of affairs is no less true in the West than it is in the East.

If we keep these very general remarks in mind (along with all of the complexity they ultimately entail), it helps clarify how a third persective between those of the United States and the Soviet Union might emerge and be brought to bear in trying to understand Solidarity. And if such a third perspective is meaningful at all, it might engender reflection and discussion that throw new light on our own self-satisfied democratic pretensions in the West. In that light we might find that the symbolic-democratic message of Solidarity is far more important than the important than the specific details and issues over which the United States and the Soviet Union bicker and about which the workers and the Polish state "try" to bargain.

Quite often our cynicism in the West about socialism leads us to reject the seriousness of the claim by socialist countries to have created a classless society. Rather than strain ourselves to "prove" that classes do indeed exist in socialist countries (an enterprise that has had many participants from Djilas onward), we might do better to accept the general claim of classlessness and proceed to understand new contradictions that exist in and pose problems for those countries. From the perspective of whether the system of production is dominated by large private ownership relations, it does indeed make sense to speak of a society like Poland as classless. That is not to say that all antagonisms, divisions, tensions, and contradictions have ceased to plague it, nor that there are not disfranchised, unfree, oppressed, and repressed members of that society caught up in various subsystems of domination and confinement. But there is a large difference between suggesting, on the one hand, that socialist ideals are mere disingenuous window dressing for the brute power of a class society that does not recognize itself as such, and, on the other hand, that a new contradiction has emerged in a society like Poland that portends a different direction for the future.

With the official abolition of class society was born a new stage of conflict and contradictions between the state, as an undemocratic, bureaucratic, technocratic instrument of the Party (not a class), and the rest of society, as an amalgamation of previous classes. What this has meant over the past half a century is that a new hegemonic force has emerged at the political level of society, forged by the dictates of the Party (Soviet and others). That political hegemony, however, has never been paralleled by developments at the level of everyday civil society, partly because of the social engineering approach of positivist Marxism. In other words, at the level of civil society the hegemonic forces of the church and other traditional elements in Polish society have engendered an inertial resistance to certain changes in political and cultural institutions and ideas.

The reason it is important to recognize the fact that the state in Poland is not the instrument of any class is that it is precisely that fact that alienates and undermines the legitimacy of political hegemony.

Put another way, if the Polish state were the instrument of a real socioeconomic class, then its political hegemony would be rooted somehow and somewhere in Polish civil society, as has been the case in previous societies. Since this is not the case, it reveals how hollow and potentially fragile the seemingly monolithic state is, and how hollow and fragile political hegemony in Poland is. The realization that the state's hegemony is somewhat like a translucent shell of legitimacy can help explain (at one level anyway) the changes that have been documented in the brief history of Solidarity.

It seems clear by now that in the beginning Solidarity emerged as a rather narrow, special-interest trade union movement with a specific axe to grind. For the most part, many of its members saw it simply as one social group in civil society against the state. But this rather pluralistic self-interpretation of the movement underwent a period of transition and transformation as the movement grew and as the state and the rest of the world responded to it. For at least a while, self-consciousness in the movement seemed to develop in a universal direction. Solidarity came to be seen internally and externally, as a social movement that represented the entire nation with the goal of demanding the conditions for a new self-governing society. Regardless of the current and future fate of Solidarity, that particular phase of its development points up perhaps its most significant movement.

The brief appointment of itself as society's representative in the face of an apparently (or potentially) paralyzed and impotent state reveals Solidarity's brief glimmer of understanding of the socially groundless character of political hegemony in Poland. This notion is crucial: if the Party's hegemony is not grounded in any larger concrete context in civil society and has only the state machinery and military as its allies and supporters (with the exception of the external "support" of the Soviet Union, of course), then the state may be much weaker or emptier than appears on the surface. Again, that is one reason why it is meaningful to analyze Solidarity's challenge in the context of a classless society. It explains the clash between Solidarity and the state in a way that truly distinguishes it from similar clashes in class societies. The distinction does not seem to be a spurious one.

Another way of addressing the issue is from the perspective of civil society and civil hegemony, from the "bottom up." One of Solidarity's demands has been that "we want to govern society and run the social system from below, where we live." This simple clarion cry for radical participatory democracy may very well arise from playing out the new contradiction between an increasingly empty set of ideological and political institutions and a growing, slowly forming, counter-hegemonic force in civil society. That new force does not constitute a rejection of socialism or of socialist ideals, but simply a demand for the concrete realization and instantiation of those ideals. This is quite different from suggesting that socialism has failed. Rather it suggests that the gap between theory and practice has been recognized and that the need to close that gap is being addressed.

In other words, it does not seem accurate to assume that the essence of the Solidarity movement is a demand for the reinstatement of the wage relationship as the arbiter of relations in the workplace, of the marketplace as the primary mediator of human relations, of production for exchange-value, of corporate society and large-scale private ownership of the productive apparatus, of class society and all that it entails, of social and economic inequality, and so on. Rather, it seems that the distilled essence of the lessons of Solidarity is the demand for the new contradiction to be resolved freely and politically: in other words, the realization of the socialist ideals of economic and social equality and justice, in conjuction with the emergence of democratic self-management, self-determination, and political autonomy. It is an old aim, but one that does not seem to be totally lost in the current endeavors of Solidarity.

In terms of our original questions, Solidarity may mean more to us than we (or they) realize. If we step outside the bipolar ideological context in which Poland finds itself trapped and deconstruct our conventional language of discourse, we may find that Solidarity represents both a demand for the democratization of everyday life inherent in the socialist program as emancipatory politics and a rebellion against all forms of instrumental, administered, bureaucratic heteronomy and the lack of collective and free control over our own destinies. These are certainly grandiose inferences to draw from the Solidarity movement and its experiences. It would be naive and wrong to assume that they have been self-consciously articulated as such or that they even reflect the real essence of that experience. But they are certainly inferences not totally unrelated to the spirit of the movement and to its objective-symbolic importance for us.

Perhaps the crucial lesson of Solidarity from a dialectical Marxist perspective is the persistent demand for radical democracy outside the usual ideological contexts of communism and capitalism. Without either surrendering the insights of the Marxist critique of current corporate capitalism or succumbing to the authoritarian and undemocratic demands of current socialist societies, we can understand the Solidarity experience as a call for new democratic theory and practice. It may be that the American model of democracy is too wedded to the beliefs of capitalism and too willing to accept procedural equality and justice as a substitute for substantive justice and equality of condition. It may also be that the Soviet model of democracy is too wedded to a rigid version of history and classless society (as ruled by the party and the positivist view of social engineering) and too willing to accept hypocrisy and cynicism in the interest of a long-range teleology.

If going beyond Solidarity can lead us to recognize the deficiencies in both models of democracy and the convergence of instrumentalist, technocratic systems of domination, then we might find ourselves on the meeting ground of a dialectical critique of both the United States and the Soviet Union. Certainly neither the United States nor the Soviet Union can take solace in these implications. Still, we must be careful not to misconstrue such highly symbolic implications as constituting the primary self-or other interpretation of Solidarity.

Perhaps the best way to conclude these ruminations is with a series of recapitulating questions. It is my hope that they can help us better frame the larger picture that is being painted in detail elsewhere in this volume. What are the symbolic implications of the new contradiction between workers and a nondemocratic bureaucratic state in the larger context of a socialist society? How do those implications point toward the concrete realization of socialist and democratic ideals in a way that is not understood in the United States and maybe not even totally by the Polish workers themselves? Is Solidarity comprehensible in terms of a new hegemonic force emerging at the level of "civil society" that finds itself in contradiction with the "political hegemony" of the state, which in turn is discovering that its hegemony and legitimation are a rather hollow shell?

Finally, we may be witnessing the earliest playing out of that new contradiction in socialist society only vaguely prefigured by the experiences of Hungary and Czechoslovakia. Are there then lessons to learn about the possibilities of a "third way" of democracy between the Scylla of pseudo-democratic, commodity-repressive, exploitative life in the United States and the Charybdis of pseudo-socialist, authoritarian, oppressive life in the Soviet Union? Do we hear echoes of a desperate cry for participatory democracy of a new sort, one not yet sufficiently understood and formulated in democratic theory or even understood totally by Solidarity itself?

These are some symbolic implications of the lessons of Solidarity. They are sadly too neglected by our discourse about that important development in human affairs. And while these are primarily suggestive and symbolic ruminations, they might yet provoke us to learn some lessons from Solidarity that transcend the historically specific context in Poland itself. If we can avoid the two views that Solidarity is either a bank of counterrevolutionary forces bent on dismantling the socialist world or a collective form of political dissidence crying for release from socialist totalitarianism, then we can begin to look beyond Solidarity. Perhaps beyond Solidarity lies a world beyond both socialism and capitalism as they are presently constituted.

10
Social Movements against the State: Theoretical Legacy of the Welfare State

Bronislaw Misztal

A new political reality marked the beginning of the 1980s, as potential conflict emerged between two social powers. States, well-organized corporate leviathans, became capable of intervening in society's organization and of implementing socioeconomic and political developments that reflected their raison d'etre. Social movements, by contrast, presented massive demands for change, based on a wide political mobilization of traditionally apathetic social layers, and became capable of effectively blocking the state's policies. It is my major premise that this conflict may become stronger and more clearly defined in the final decades of the twentieth century. Although conflict exists in both the West and the East, it would be a gross theoretical exaggeration to ascribe similar causes to observed contradictions. The question is whether contemporary theory is prepared to explain these conflictual differences.

The developments of the early 1980s in Poland, West Germany, and elsewhere took sociology by surprise. In addition to the fact that these unprecedented urban political movements could not be explained by existing theories, the whole ontological system of contemporary sociology, split into schools, disciplines, and fields, was unprepared to describe and comprehend the set of phenomena that crossed the traditional boundaries of academic disciplines. This ontological handicap occurred in four major areas.

First, the theory of the state, as provided by political sociology has remained relatively underdeveloped (Crouch 1979, 13-24) and has only recently focused on the macrosocial determinants of state power (Badie and Birnbaum 1983; Poulantzas 1978; Therborn 1980). Second, despite the fact that its origin could be traced to the 1930s, the theory of social movements has remained immature, mostly as an inescapable element of the collective behavior approach (Smelser 1963). The theory has only recently broken with this tradition (Roberts and Klos 1979), but its search for intel-

143

lectual alliances remains quite unclear theoretically, despite the introduction of a somewhat fresher approach (Touraine 1981). Third, urban sociology itself has remained irrelevant with regard to emerging forms of massive struggle, subscribing to the unsubstantiated view that every such struggle is simply one more case of "persistent urban social problems" (Gold 1981). At the other extreme, however it has developed a distorted political perspective (Castells 1977) that has led an the overgeneralization of social relations of consumption (Harloe 1979, 153). Only recently have new perspectives on the state reached and politicized urban sociology, but the orthodox Marxist character of the "urban question" approach (ibid.) has prevented wider theoretical discourse. Fourth, political economy, although addressing the complex relationship between state interventionism and the spontaneity of economic development (Brus 1972, 1973), has yet to develop a more critical attitude toward the mode of production of social inequalities in the city (Szelenyi 1983). Until recently, this sort of research has not been effectively linked with the macrosocial determinants of urban social movements (Misztal and Misztal 1984a).

For the past ten to twenty years the four disciplines--political sociology, social movements theory, urban sociology, and political economy--have remained largely unrelated. While political sociology and economy has oscillated between issues other than new and powerful emerging state, theories of social movements and urban sociology have avoided politicization. In the meantime, however, two opposite processes have gradually been dominating social reality: the increasing appetite and power of the interventionist state and the increasing desire of civil societies to take responsibility for development into their own hands.

Political Sociology and Theories of the State

Twentieth-century political sociology has been dominated by the Weberian and Marxian traditions. The Weberian view focused on such issues as the "means of administration," "mode of government," and the "monopoly of legitimate physical force" (Badie and Birnbaum 1983, 16-20). The Marxian tradition indicated some cognitive dualism. It stressed "the state's genuine independence from civil society as a whole and from the bourgeoisie as a ruling class" (ibid., 10), and a reduction of state power to the economic power of the ruling class (ibid.). Subsequently, the "secondariness of the state with respect to the economy" dominated the Marxian tradition and did away with the "state versus civil society" approach (Nowak 1983, 138). Both major traditions came to be dominated by nonbasic elements of their founders' thought. Since, however, these traditions have become part of the dominant ideologies in both the West and the East, they have influenced, legitimized, and explained two major trends in the state's development. (Therborn 1980, 172)

The first trend, deriving from the Weberian tradition and further informed by the functionalist view, led from the "neofunctionalist model of the state" to the "welfare state." The academic analysis of the state evolved toward a distinction between the spheres of private social relations and public authority (Badie and Birnbaum 1983, 26). The highly acclaimed modernization of the state through increased differentiation, autonomization, universalization, and institutionalization was perceived as responsible for this evolution (ibid. 27). The intermediate stages of the "negative state" (economic liberalism) and the "positive state" (limited interventionism) were identified as the supposed road toward some form of "democratic socialism" (Macridis 1983, 39). The notion and practice of the "welfare state" are crucial to an understanding of the nature of the conflict between movements and the state organization. The most concise definition identifies the "welfare state" as a sort of "socialization of the costs of reproducing labor power and the use of state policy to alter the distribution of rewards and opportunities by the market mechanisms of the capitalist economy" (Pontusson 1983, 48). Transfer payments (taxation and social security) and the public provision of social services (commodities) are major forms of state activity. The tasks of the socialization of labor costs and distribution of rewards involve the state in the interventionist mode that focuses on providing "the good life for the individual" (Furness and Tilton 1979, 2). There are, however, certain features of this interventionism that may indeed alter and distort the role of the state.

Above all, political theory has noted that instead of providing the good life for the individual, the state has tended to focus on providing the "good life for the state" (Furniss and Tilton 1979, 4). The new focus may stem either from the alienation of the protective role of the state or from the evolution of individual and societal needs ultimately at odds with what was formerly acknowledged by the state; the divergent perceptions of the military security issue between state officials and societal representatives in West Germany is an example. Frequently, both processes take place, further widening the gap between the interventionist and protectionist appetites of the state and the libertarian feelings of the populace. Another feature of interventionism under the welfare state is that the latter does not change the basic sources of inequality. Instead, the state aims at altering the effects of inequality, while the roots remain untouched (Pontusson 1983, 49). Although it is not inconceivable a society may opt for substantial sociopolitical and/or economic reconstruction while the state remains committed to its original task of smoothing the conflict instead of resolving it, political theory has seldom tackled this problem.

Subsequently, modes of interventionism may evolve through which the state extends its "territorial waters" and thereby improves its own position. Pontusson (1983) identifies three major criteria to classify the modes of intervention. First, the state may intervene in the sphere of production, distribution, or in both. Second, state intervention, when governed by selective criteria, may either prevent or promote certain social processes. Third, the state may intervene either through capital or labor markets (ibid., 50-51). Theoretically, it is possible to imagine a situation in which state intervention takes a more and more coordinated and total form. This interrelation of state and economy serves to reproduce the existing sociopolitical arrangement, which is often mistakenly interpreted as "the reproduction of society" (Therborn 1980, 164). The aim of this reproduction, however, becomes a complicated superstructural polity rather than society.

The capitalist state, evolving toward a more elaborate model of multidimensional interventionism, exercises the principal political control over the economy through the processes of production and distribution. The state potentially may extend its control beyond the limits of welfare and commodity provision and infringe upon the autonomy of societal values. A model of the relationship between the state and society thus evolves. The state, traditionally restricted to the political sphere, develops welfare functions that also enable it to penetrate the societal sphere. This evolution has been best interpreted by Hirsh (1983), who has analyzed the recent situation in West Germany. The emerging "security state" guarantees "both the material survival of its social members as well as their functional adjustment and regulation, their social conditioning and surveillance" (ibid., 78-79). The state apparatus, according to Hirsch, extends deep into the social organism, develops a bureaucratic network of regulation and control, and replaces the natural social structures with "statified" controlling agencies. The notion of intervention becomes less and less relevant. Instead, the state slowly merges into the societal sphere, loosening its directly repressive grip and strengthening its indirect and overwhelming surveillance over societal values. Even the fusion of a socialist government with capitalist state structures as in France, can lead to a peculiar corporatization of the system, excluding labor movement organization and promoting social reforms through the existing antidemocratic institutions of the state (Kesselman 1983).

One set of possible explanations for this complex process of "statization" of societies, with its increasing autonomy of state power and the corporatization of democracy, may be the numerical growth, programmatic vagueness and political weakness of the middle class, which ultimately lead this class to strive for an increase in its own security. This increase in security is gained by curtailing labor's appetites to control its own social destiny or "historicity" (Bertaux 1977; Touraine, 1981). In other words, the increased autonomization of state power, when it takes place, is realized in the name of increased security and stability. But this trend in fact brings about the political establishment of a new middle class that seeks control over society through the increased surveillance function of the state.

Developments in other types of sociopolitical systems also indicate growing tensions between state and society. In Poland, for example, the emerging postindustrial civil society (Arato 1981, 27) was a response to the increasing autonomy of state authority in outlining developmental strategies. While state authority was trying to preserve its monopoly on the articulation of development programs, society, was growing increasingly concerned about the rightness of the state's value systems. Here again, one sees the legacy of the socialist welfare state through which the scope of the state's intervention became magnified as a result of its earlier policy of social consumption provision (Misztal and Misztal 1984b). When several crises reduced the scale of social consumption provision, the state apparatus continued to survey the spheres in which potential unrestrained response was possible, by imposing restrictions on both labor organization and the creation of values (both within the societal sphere) and simultaneously protecting the organization of industry. Society, however, defended its right to respond spontaneously whenever the state's developmental policies failed or were vague. This debate continued while the state attempted to depoliticize the societal sphere and reduce it further to the private sphere (Habermas 1973, 42). Only the emergence of the Solidarity movement reversed this process, but an escalation of the conflict resulted.

The aggravated conflict between state and society produced mixed theoretical responses within political sociology. The growth of the state became a major concern. This growth occurred in both the West and the East, but the structural causes of the growth in state autonomization, as well as the ways in which autonomization manifested itself, were different. It is impossible to understand these structural causes without further elaborating on urban social movements and urban inequalities. The specific relationships among social movements, the state political system, and the determinants of urban social inequality indicate that although the legacy of the welfare state in both political systems influenced the perspective of sociological theory, its impact was based on ontologically distinct patterns.

Theory of Social Movements

Social movements have seldom been seriously treated by sociological theory. Though one can defend the argument that some type of social movement has always underlain major political breakdowns, revolutions, and changes, Turner and Killian (1957) attributed the origins of massive social commotion to episodes of collective behavior (Lang and Lang 1961). American sociology has, thus established a mistaken tradition of viewing social movements as unorganized mass behavior. As Heberle (1979, vii) has pointed out: "This approach stems from an essentially conservative, status quo, accepting phase in American sociology." In defense of the existing social order, sociological theory became interested in "structural conduciveness" (Smelser 1963), seeing social conditions as facilitating the outburst of collective action. Such action was frightening, potentially unpredictable, and had to be dealt with through a series of instrumental measures that would control the crowd, curb the spontaneity of developments, and bring about the restabilization of the social order (Rush and Denisoff 1971). Even this limited approach acknowledged some degree of social change stemming from the successful end of a cycle: order-turmoil-social order. Both the "collective behavior" approach and the later "social revolutions" approach (Davies 1962; Brinton 1952), however, focused on either the failures of the system or the conditions leading to an outburst, not on the nature of the conflict that made people protest. From this perspective, the avoidance of agitation and social movement was a function of the adaptational capacity of the system, since social turmoil resulted from imperfect social organization, fragmented social control, or economic deprivation. Should social organization be improved, control restored, or deprivation lessened, neither massive movements nor major revolutions would occur.

This perspective was apparently reassuring. The conception of the welfare state was therefore seen as the only logical response to the uncertainty brought about by social development. The image of the state as being willingly responsible for the socialization of the costs of reproducing labor had a soothing effect on sociologists and politicians. The state was to be the intermediary between the demands of society and the outcomes of spontaneous socioeconomic development. Nobody would be blamed for the increasing costs of development, but the state would get the credit for solving social problems or for managing crises. In the case of a disruptive breakdown within the economy or the polity, the state--the welfare state--would be responsible for elaborating new programs and for their implementation and social approval. Since the state was not to be blamed for any dysfunctions of social development, even in the case of massive social movements (such as the student revolts of the 1960s), the nature of the conflict was not clear. The function of social movements was to challenge the culture, or the system of values and beliefs, but the state was spared confrontation. The programmatic content of social movements did not challenge the state, nor did sociological analyses attribute such challenging attempts to social movements. On the whole, Western sociological theories of social movements avoided the perception of major conflict. Even when the social movements built barricades, the question of who was barricaded was not entirely clear to the theoreticians.

The 1970s brought about a major breakthrough in sociological perspectives on social movements, producing more elaborate sociological analyses focused on political aspects of the movements (Kriesberg 1973). First, it became clear that social movements are often "attempts at changing power and order" (Roberts and Klos 1979, 14) and that they are directed toward structural or ideological change (Ash 1972). Second, after the functionalist and neopositivist approaches (Smelser 1963) failed to explain the structural causes of social movements (as distinct from collective behavior), sociologists turned to radical, conflict, and Marxist approaches in search of some logical explanation. It became apparent that while capitalism has a tendency to turn every human being into an economic commodity, social movements vigorously oppose this tendency (Roberts and Klos 1979, 20). Therefore, the major arenas in which social movements are expected to manifest themselves are those through which the commodity fetishism of the capitalist state is implemented. For cautious Marxists like Roberts and Klos, the principal trends giving rise to social movements were industrialization, bureaucratization, and imperialization.

Although recent approaches part company with the tradition of "collective behavior," there is little theoretical knowledge about the reasons social movements emerge, the values they defend, and their contribution to the progress and development of social systems. Neither the Hegelian (rather than Marxian) dialectic of social change, nor the trends and movements noted by Roberts and Klos (ibid., 15) explains why, for example, industrialization sometimes produces egalitarian movements, why such movements are sometimes directed against industrialization, or why they turn against the system that promotes industrialization as a means of development. Is the statement that "social movements [in contrast to collective behavior] occur only in certain kinds of societies, . . . [that is] hardly possible in totalitarian regimes" (Heberle 1979) the only available generalization about social movements?

The question is: if social movements are indeed collective enterprises to restructure power and order relations within society, against what are they ultimately directed? At this point, I believe, the sociological theory of social movements discovers the state and its impact on contemporary society.

While social movements may be credited with attempting to bring about the restructuring of power, states focus on ensuring the stability and organization of social life, thereby preserving the power order. The opposition of interests between states and social movements is not a functional necessity, however, throughout history, states were an organizational form of response "that some . . . societies were forced to make to an increasing division of labor coupled with strong resistance to social change" on the part of certain social classes (Badie and Birnbaum 1983, 135).

So long as the state can foster a strategy of controlled change, evolution, and progress, it is able to control society without a major challenge on the part of social movements. Crucial to this process of social control is the monopolization of the production of ideas and their institutionalization in the form of ideology. The power-wielding process, as a tool to exert social control, may be based either on the principles of democracy or on authoritarianism, but as long as the state does not impede historical development its position as the organizational superstructure of society is not threatened. In other words, from a purely functional viewpoint, an enlightened state monopoly would be possible if it did not interfere with the historical process.

Bureaucratization of the process through which development is managed restricts ideas of progress to those conceived by the administrative structures of the state. In other words, the state monopolizes developmental policies, presumably in search of a more effective and less distorted operation. To justify, legitimize, and "cover" this increased professionalization of state policy-making, two means may be employed. One is the institutionalization of democratic mechanisms, through which the state seeks society's approval for its monopolistic position. Processes such as negotiation, representation, and the articulation of interests are supposed to widen citizen participation and help solve political problems at the lower levels of bargaining, without the cumulated mobilization of society. But the democratic remedy is effective only so long as society is willing to recognize the state's privileged position in setting the goals of development or so long as there is no crucial issue that polarizes the two elements (as represented by some form of societal organization). The other remedy is the socialization of the whole process of economic development, widely called socialism. Such processes as the "proliferation of officials" (Weber 1916, 1978, 259) are supposed to widen the delegation of power through the further bureaucratization of state-society relationships and help depoliticize economic problems by making bargaining redundant. The demobilization of society is the intended result. In both cases the production of ideas and the implementation of ideology are put aside; and the state is allowed to operate without being challenged by a mobilized society.

The social movements that have emerged in the second half of the twentieth century, however, have a different scope, since they are the "organized collective behavior of a class actor struggling against his class adversary" (Touraine 1981, 77). The increased demands of societies to have more say over the philosophy of development, rather than over the real course of developmental policies, have caused modern social movements to couple idea production with organized proceedings for social change. The quality and quantity of such idea production are distinctively new (as illustratd by the Polish and West German examples) and satisfy the demands of society, but they are at the same time unacceptable to governments acting as states' representatives.

In a sense, both social movements and states attempt to satisfy societies by offering some exclusive "prescriptions" for social development. The state's prescription, political in itself, is rational and contains such elements as tradition, security, raison d'etat, and political order. The movement's prescription, on the other hand, is more emotional and contains such elements as the "good life for society" (as opposed to the "good life for the state"), new structures of societal values, goals beyond the abilities of traditional democratic capitalism or bureaucratic socialism, and, more and more frequently, a new political philosophy.

Conflictual relationships between social movements and states result from their mutual tendency to extend control over society by the use of ideas of social change. Society, however, is searching to free itself from organizational and ideological ties. This quest for identity, subjectivity, and control over historicity (Touraine 1981) will further position society in the center of conflict, juxtaposing the state and social movements.

There is little doubt that within the past decade newly emerging issues of societal concern have played, and will continue to play, a crucial role in placing the state in opposition to society. Mobilizing society's members to struggle for these new goals creates a peculiar situation, however, in which two highly organized "social products" (i.e., the state and social movements) compete for control over society. There is, as I see it, an antithetical relationship between them which is best expressed by the fact that states attempt to maintain the status quo through monopolizing developmental policies, while social movements attempt to bring about social change in exactly the same way.

The major problem stemming from this analysis is the quality and direction of social change, development, and progress. Can developmental policies be carried out and can they turn into the qualitative progress while the state and social movements are involved in conflict? What is the cost of such a conflict for the society involved? Two situations are possible here. Some mediating institutions are conceived and implemented to solve the conflict or else some measures of austerity may be adopted to suppress the adversary. Either measure can be adopted by social movements or by the state. This creates four hypothetical situations in which the conflict may be carried out.

The most interesting situation is a combination that occurs when the mediation measures adopted by one party are coupled with the austerity measures adopted by the other party. For example, consociational steps adopted by the state, coupled with challenges by the movement, could lead to a more theoretically distinctive political solution than the combination of austerity measures adopted by the state coupled with consociational policies advocated by the movement.

New Urban Sociology and the Concept of the State

For many years urban sociology was the least politicized field of sociological inquiry, so that conflicts emerging in society (capitalist society) were either neglected (Pickvance 1983) or interpreted in peculiar, apolitical ways (see Jaret 1983). This resulted from the ontological premises on which "old" urban sociology was based. The concepts of urban sociology were traditionally drawn "from a consensus model of a society whose rationale is that the needs of the individual are compatible with the needs of society"

(Pickvance 1983, 19). In this context, the central authority, or the state, appears as a relatively neutral organization acting in the general interest to restore or ensure social equilibrium. The traditional distinction between urban and rural also contributed to a delineation of the "urban question" so that was perceived as being in opposition to industrial and economic (ibid.). The research questions generated by "old" urban sociology dealt with what were seen as threats to the existing system of social order by unrestrained social processes such as immigration.

Traditional urban sociology thus placed itself above it all, as on a balcony. The balcony is "the symbol of reaction, conservatism, and status quo. It may be the privileged position of the snug elites in the old regime who do not seem to understand what may be going on down on the streets" (Roberts and Klos 1979, 1). While urban sociology was not far from the city streets, it usually regarded developments on those streets from the secure perspective of the balcony. From that perspective the visible aspects of collective human behavior looked like social unrest aimed against the existing social order. A look across the balcony however, revealed the stabilizing influence of the state.

By contrast, the new urban sociology with a predominantly Marxist (Pickvance 1983) and neo-Marxist (Jaret 1983) orientation, was drawn from the conflict model of society. Subsequently, the opposition between the state represented by the capitalist economy, and society, represented by the class organizations, emerged as a crucial relationship characterizing contemporary capitalist society. While the traditional perspective took for granted the protective aspects of the welfare state, the Marxist perspective saw the state as reflecting the class struggle, whether through the organization of the political interests of the dominant class or through regular economic intervention (Lojkine 1977). State involvement also affected the growing scope of social consumption (Castells 1977). A somewhat mechanical conclusion followed: through its arrangement of space the state became the real manager of everday life and the emerging social issues became the subject of urban social movements (urban struggles).

This simplistic interpretation was based on intuition rather than on an elaborated body of theoretical knowledge. By rejecting the consensual perspective on society, urban sociology left its balcony and went in search of the reasons for the polarization of society. Instead of looking for structural conditions that would explicate the issues crucial to a specific type of conflict, urban sociology pointed to the immediately visible characteristics of urban collective behavior as if they were indispensable of conflict. As noted by Harloe (1979, 142), the argument about the crucial "role of urban social movements and urban contradictions as a potentially important area for revolutionary political activity" was not so much wrong as theoretically unsubstantiated. Harloe's critical examination of the relationship between the state and the "urban question" in those early Marxist approaches indicates their "remarkable similarity" to the bourgeois theories, since both types fall short of theoretical and real objectives, containing instead an ideological fuse (ibid., 128). The functionalist view of urban politics results from this analysis (ibid., 142).

Thus, neither approach in urban sociology has been able to overcome the ontological dilemma (Sztompka 1979), since the role of the state has remained unclear and disputable. This is why Castells' argument that "the development of community organizations and urban protest movements" in the United States constituted a "challenge to the established social-spatial division of labor and consumption" was poorly received (1976, 14). In his otherwise interesting analysis of the unrestrained processes in a capitalist city, Castells was unable to relate urban crisis properly to the development of a qualitatively new type of state. His emphasis on the "process of capitalist accumulation," as well as the "organization of socialized consumption" and the "reproduction of the social order," did not grasp the essence of the conflict (ibid., 13). As a result, a theoretically weak picture of urban social movements emerged. The movements were supposed to respond directly to the failure of urban policies to handle the problems generated by uneven urban-suburban development (ibid.). A simplistic vision of social movements was thus adopted to explain a multi-dimensional urban crisis. In this vision the movements were simply responses to the stimulus of mismanagement and the breakdown of services, not a new form of social action. These movements further antagonized the state, mostly at the local level, causing the state to lose "control over the social conflicts growing up from the urban issues" (ibid., 21).

This backwards perspective has long dominated urban sociology, overshadowing the fact that the state "needed" more urban conflicts to restructure its organization and gain a larger degree of relative autonomy (Szelenyi 1981). The belief that the principal social transformations occur solely on the societal level and that the state only confronts challenges passively (clearly a losing battle) was wishful thinking. In reality, transformations occur simultaneously on societal and political levels. The fiscal crisis of the cities was merely a symptom of the restructuring of the relations of ownership in capitalist society. If

Castells' premise were valid, the transformation of the welfare state into the security state (Hirsch 1983) would be seen as a forced weakening of the state apparatus, but in reality it strengthened the state's social control. Social movements thus have been perceived more as struggles (i.e., immediate conflicts between the urban folk and the local administration) than as elements in a contradictory set-up in which society and the state contend for the monopolization of development programs. Consequently, urban sociology's approach to social movements has had little theoretical importance: by mistaking the result for the causal factor, it diverted attention from the real contradictory relationship.

Urban sociology has also made an unfortunate distinction between the socialist and the capitalist city (Hill 1976). Although the "State Capitalist City" emerged as "an integral unit of corporate state capitalism," (ibid., 43), it was also believed that the "Socialist City" directed its produced surplus to the residents, thus becoming "the urban-political foundation" for socialist society (ibid., 47). This ontological step practically eliminated the possibility of recognizing urban social movements under state socialism that derived from contradictory relations within the socialist state itself. According to such an interpretation, social movements were urban struggles in the capitalist city, but they could be considered little better than riots if they took place in the socialist city. The structure and causes of such movements were not thus explicated by urban sociology. It has only recently been proven that cities under socialism also suffer inequalities and that those inequalities are neither inherited from the capitalist past nor maintained by surviving market mechanisms or other re-emerging forces of capitalism (Szelenyi 1983, 4). The problem of contradictions intrinsic to the urban sphere have been formulated in the following way:

> "while under capitalism the market creates the basic inequalities and the administrative allocation of welfare modifies and moderates them slightly, under socialism the major inequalities are created by administrative allocation, and the market can be used to reduce inequalities"
> (ibid., 11).

Since the market is not used to alleviate large scale social problems in the socialist city, unrestrained social processes emerge (Misztal and Misztal 1984b), causing spontaneous societal responses almost identical to those occurring in the capitalist "wild city" (Castells 1976).

There is an apparent ontological gap between the "new" urban sociology's approach to the capitalist city and the Marxist approach to the socialist city. Specific structural conditions differ in both types of urban realities, as do the mechanisms that govern them. Apart from these structural determinants, however, it can be observed that restraints of inequality are similar, as are the spontaneous societal responses.

The theoretical weakness of urban sociology results from the inconsistency of the methodological premises upon which it is based. On the one hand, it is willing to point to structural determinants that govern the distribution of capital through space as the factor responsible for urban struggles and subsequent movements. On the other hand, urban sociology is reluctant to accept the determining role of administrative allocation that governs the distribution of facilities and privileges through the urban space under socialism. This internal inconsistency actually depoliticizes urban sociology, since it dissociates structural conduciveness (to social movements) from the transformations experienced by the state.

In particular it blurs is the character of urban struggles, since there is no apparent relation between the objectivized interest and the distribution-allocation issue. Limited attempts to overcome this theoretical weakness focus on "the revolutionary potential of sociospatial praxis as something complementary to the class struggle" (Gottdiener 1984, 22). From this perspective "independent and spontaneous collective actions which have re-asserted the primacy of social space over property exchange values acquire great significance" (ibid.). While the "collective consumption" approach actually reduces political collective episodes to the rank of merely economic responses to unequal commodity provisions, this "sociospatial" perspective provides recognition of the cultural contents of the space.

Unfortunately, the major issue--that of the relationship between the state and the city, or betweeen the polity and the urban sphere--remains obscure. Why the major struggle in contemporary society takes place in the sociospatial setting of the city and why the class interests of the state are best realized in the form of control over urban development are still not clear. In effect, developments within the state and processes within the urban community are unrelated, until an attempt is made to renegotiate or redefine patterns of inequality and development programs. In this context, urban society is <u>de facto</u> reduced to a subjective role, and the line is drawn between the deprived (or dominated) urban folk and the privileged (or dominating) economic machinery.

Political Economy and the Interrelation Between the State and Social Movements

The theoretical scope and explanatory ability of political economy, although intuitively acceptable to scholars operating within the traditional epistemological framework of Marxist inquiry (Brus 1973, 86), have seldom been analyzed as to applicability to interdisciplinary research. The multiple meanings attributed to political economy are the reason for the limited use of this approach, as pointed out by Walton (1979, 6-7). In fact, political economy has been perceived as both a tool for neo-Marxist criticism of production, distribution, and exchange (O'Connor 1976, 17), and as a means to analyze public policy. The contemporary social sciences, however, political economy is being "discovered" as a "theoretical perspective... concerned with holistic explanations of social inequality" (Walton 1979, 8). At this point the political economic approach has crossed the borders of political and urban sociology and penetrated the field of social movements' theory.

In all three areas of inquiry the scholar encounters persistent problems in attempting to explain social inequality. Whereas the state may be considered a supplier of public goods and services, a regulator of the marketplace operation, an intervening factor that achieves its own policy objectives, or an arbiter among social groups (Clark and Dear 1982, 49), the issue of who benefits remains crucial. No answer is possible without considering political economy. When capitalist or socialist urban problems are considered, the question remains whether the similarity of "certain common problems stemming from industrialization" (Walton 1979, 12) result from structurally similar patterns of inequality or not.

In his analysis of the industrial crisis, Crouch (1979, 23) has indicated that the structure of inequality is directly related to the role of the state, to relationships between economic domination and the workforce, and to "the extent to which the work force is collectivized and the relationship of its organs to both economic domination and the state" (ibid., 14). This puts political economy at the center of theoretical analysis of state-society relations. Such a sociological interpretation of political economy confronts three classes of problems. It deals first with the strategy of resource allocation, second, with the political order, and third, with the mode of subordinates' organization. Each class of problems produces inherent dilemmas, and, according to the way those dilemmas are solved, certain structural types of inequality emerge.

The dilemmas characteristic of resource allocation include equity versus objectivity, administration versus emergence, systematic versus ad hoc determination, and growth versus redistribution (Crouch 1979, 23-25). The dilemmas facing the political order include the character of both the state (i.e., coercive or noncoercive; active or passive) and the power structure (class or officialdom), which provide guidelines for resource allocation (ibid., 19-20; Bauman 1974, 142-47). On the most encompassing level (the organization of subordinates) emerging dilemmas determine the dimension of entities subject to resource allocation. As pointed out by Crouch (1979, 21-22), subordinates may be regarded as individualized or collectivized, heteronomous or autonomous in relation to modes of allocation and power and deriving their existence from the state or civil society.

The major ontological question still remains: Can capitalist and socialist social reality be described using the same theory or similar theoretical focus? While in the case of the three earlier fields of inquiry (political sociology of the state, social movements theory, and political urban sociology) the apparent advantage was on the side of the research on capitalist society, but the case of political economy indicates that the analysis of socialist society may unveil answers to problems raised by the other fields. The key problems in these fields are as follows:

1. How safe is the state's growing independence from society, and how is the statization of social life dealt with in both capitalism and socialism?
2. Given the increase in welfare and security functions assumed by the state, how much the societal discontent embodied by the new social movements will be directed against the urban mode of production of social inequalities and/or the state itself in both capitalism and socialism?
3. How much of the increase in urban social inequalities can be credited to excessive interventionism and how much results from the post-industrial mode of development of both capitalism and socialism?

The political economic approach sheds light on the third issue in particular. Pointing to the fact that socialist society is a "post-capitalist" form, Nowak (1983, 222) presupposes that the cessation of traditional class struggle leaves even more room for uncontrolled state intervention. "When the mechanism of solving crises by the masses is stopped, the only way to save the system becomes the increase of state consumption. And the state following its own material interest sooner or later begins to intervene in economic life" (ibid.); this situation is known as the Rosa Luxemburg problem. Political economy, suggests a solution that points to the distinct structural conditions that differentiate socialism from capitalism. It does not suggest a lack of class struggle, but instead a new form of struggle is between the "disposers of coercion" (ibid.) and the civil society (Crouch 1977, 23). Of the six different ideal types of solutions to class conflict and the crisis of industrial relations crises (market individualism; dominant or subordinate liberal collectivism; and statist, voluntarist, and private corporatism), two models become subject negotiation and bargaining. In the case of capitalism, a compromise solution focuses on "productivity bargaining" and its departure point is that of private corporatism. (ibid., 63), effect there is an "attempt at restoring order, increasing involvement and treating conflicts as matters of rights, at the expense of certain risk in extending the scope of pluralism" (ibid., 61). The compromise solution brings about an increase in productivity, the rise of managerialism, and the strengthened role of ideology in the control of labor.

In the case of socialism, a compromise solution focuses on order and redistributive bargaining, departing from the model of state corporatism. The state attempts to negotiate public approval for order and also down plays the role of consultation. This leads to a peculiar situation, since negotiation or bargaining takes place only when subordinates are exercising power; when they do not, there is very little contact between authorities and the labor force (Crouch 1977 16; Morawski 1983). With the lack of ideological consensus, the emerging conflicts are interpreted as clashes of interests and resolved through a test of power, either by a crackdown on the opposition or by forcing it to compromise. The heteronomous situation of labor is paradoxical, om that dominant class interests are imposed in the name of the proletariat. The state is the sole controlling agent to decide upon the existence of collectivities, that derive their rights from the state itself. Inequality is the product of administrative decisions imposed from above, not emerging from a process of socioeconomic interaction, and is further supported by attempts at systematic social planning. Under economic constraints and stagnation, social policy focuses the redistribution of wealth at the expense of allegedly privileged groups (Misztal 1981). During prosperity however, the state fosters policies which promise unlimited increases in the level of general wealth, since aspirational deprivation (Morrison 1971, 103-15) increases societal manageability and draws attention to the goal of consumerism (Morawski 1983, 215).

The responses to the compromise presented by both capitalist and socialist societies, differ significantly. Crouch (1977, 66) has pointed to the fact that the most common response under capitalism is for labor movements to seek a more orthodox pattern of bargaining, which is characteristic of dominant liberal collectivism. It focuses on negotiating inequality issues (pay increases) in exchange for diminished conflict. There is little doubt that such a compromise "has no important implications for the role of the State" (ibid., 63). The "pay-off" model of compromise brings labor under the direct control of capital, this is the major point of the political economic approach. This means that bargaining parties agree to share, however inequally, the results of increased productivity and to redistribute existing wealth slightly.

The structure of compromise under state socialism is completely different. Morawski (1983, 218-25) has indicated that by the time primary industrialization was completed, bureaucratic state socialism had been discredited. The intermediate compromise is still evident in Czechoslovakia and East Germany. It took the form of technocratic socialism and had many features of voluntarist corporatism whereby employers, together with the noncoercive state, constituted the source of authority (Crouch 1977, 43). With the failure of the redistributive and productive capacities of such a model of "existing socialism," unions focused on further neutralizing the state by compelling employers to accept bargaining. These attempts, however unsuccessful in Poland in 1980-1981, raised questions as to the mobilizational mechanisms employed by the state and thus contributed to the emergence of conflict between state and society.

This leads to the conclusion that the increase in urban social inequality is entirely due to the socialist state's excessive interventionism, which has resulted from the past failures of bureaucratic welfare socialism. The legacy of the welfare state under capitalism, by contrast, does not lead to precisely such a conclusion, since the scope of political and social crises differs within countries under that system (Cherki et al. 1978, 274). After all the "final resolution of conflict depends to a substantial extent on the kind of relationship which exists between central and local authorities, the political orientation of the dominant establishment and the degree with which the political system allows open expression" (ibid., 272).

One may further conclude that social movements under capitalism are more likely to turn against certain models of production (Szelenyi 1981, 589) than directly against the state itself, since the institution of state is shielded behind a wider political and legal structure. State socialism, however removes the shield by virtue of the protective and welfare functions exerted directly by the state apparatus and expected by society. Consequently, the state apparatus under socialism becomes a target for renegotiating the compromise solution. While the failure of welfare provision under capitalism can be blamed on intermediary structures, under state socialism, the failure is directly credited to the state's inefficiency. As indicated by Birnbaum (1983, 43), this structural difference creates various types of mobilization which, when coupled with the specific form of the state, may make the state more vulnerable to challenges by the movement. The enormous centralizaion of state power (ibid.) in France (Kesselman 1983) and Poland (Morawski 1983) further strengthens both arguments.

A final conclusion is that statization of social life, as demonstrteded by Nowak (1983, 222), stems from structurally divergent conditions that govern state-society relations under socialism and capitalism Only the dualism of class struggle focuses society's attention on the overwhelming presence of the apparatus of the socialist state (Bauman 1974), thus upgrading the scale of conflict. The contradiction between the libertarian collectivist attitudes of society and the corporatist attitudes of the state makes this conflict inevitable. The statization of social life under capitalism is more tolerable to society, because the structures of the state itself remain intact even when a compromise delivers less than the original goals. In effect, collectivist compromise inevitably accompanies the state's evolution from welfare to security functions.

REFERENCES

Arato, Andrew. 1981. "Civil Society Against the State: Poland 1980-81." Telos 47 (Spring).
Ash, Roberta. 1982. Social Movements in America. Chicago: Markham.
Badie, Bertrand and Pierre, Birnbaum. 1983. The Sociology of the State. Chicago: University of Chicago Press.
Bauman, Zygmunt. 1974. "Officialdom and Class: Bases of Inequality in Socialist Society." F. Parkin, ed. The Social Analysis of Class Structure. London: Tavistock.
Bertaux, Daniel. 1977. Destins personnels et structures de classe. Paris: Presses Universitaires de France.
Birnbaum, Pierre. 1983. "Mobilizations, structures sociales et types d' Etat." Revue Francaise de Sociologie, 24, No. 3.
Brinton, Crane. 1952. Anatomy of Revolution. New York: Vintage Books.
Brus, Wlodzimierz. 1972. The Market in a Socialist Economy. London: Routledge & Kegan Paul.
────────. 1973. The Economics and Politics of Socialism. London: Routledge & Kegan Paul.
Castells, Manuel. 1976. "The Wild City." Kapitalistate 4/5.
────────. 1977. The Urban Question. Cambridge, Mass.: MIT Press.
Cherki, Eddie et al. 1978. "Urban Protest in Western Europe." C. Crouch and A. Pizzorno, eds. The Resurgence of Class Conflict in Western Europe Since 1968 2. New York: Holmes & Meier.
Clark, Gordon, and Michael Dear. 1981. "The State in Capitalism and the Capitalist State." A. Scott and M. Dear, eds. Urbanization and Urban Planning in Capitalist Society. London: Methuen.
Crouch, Colin. 1977. Class Conflict and the Industrial Relations Crisis. London: Heineman.
────────. ed. 1979. State and Economy in Contemporary Capitalism. London: Croom Helm.
Davies, James C. 1962. "Toward a Theory of Revolution." American Sociological Review 27.
Furniss, Norman and Timothy Tilton. 1979. The Case for the Welfare State. Bloomington: Indiana University Press.
Giddens, Anthony. 1979. Central Problems in Social Theory. Berkeley: University of California Press.
Gold, Harry. 1982. The Sociology of Urban Life. Englewood Cliffs, N.J.: Prentice-Hall.

Gottdiener, Mark. "The Debate on the Theory of Space: Towards an Urban Praxis." M. Smith, ed. Capital, Class and Urban Structure. [Forthcoming]. Quoted from the manuscript with author's consent.
Habermas, Jurgen. 1973. La technique et la science comme ideologie. Paris: Galimard.
Harloe, Michael. 1979. "Marxism, the state and the urban question: critical notes on two recent French theories." C. Crouch, ed. State and Economy in Contemporary Capitalism. London: Croom Helm, Heberle, Rudolf. 1979. "Foreword." R. E. Roberts and R. M. Klos. Social Movements: Between the Balcony and the Barricade. St. Louis, Mo.: Mosby.
Hill, Richard C. 1976. "Fiscal crisis and political struggle in the decaying U.S. central city." Kapitalistate 4/5.
Hirsch, Joachim. 1983. "Fordist Security State and New Social Movements." Kapitalistate 10/11.
Jaret, Charles. 1983. "Recent neo-marxist urban analysis." Annual Review of Sociology 9.
Jenkins, Craig J. 1983. "Resource Mobilization Theory and the Study of Social Movements." Annual Review of Sociology 9.
Kesselman, Mark. 1983. "France: Socialism Without the Workers." Kapitalistate 10/11.
Kriesberg, Louis, ed. 1973. Research in Social Movements, Conflict and Change. Greenwich, Conn.: JAI Press.
Lang, Kurt and Gladys Lang. 1961. Collective Dynamics. New York: Thomas Crowell.
Lojkine, Jean. 1977. Le Marxisme, l'Etat et la Question Urbaine. Paris: PUF.
Macridis, Roy C. 1983. Contemporary Political Ideologies: Movements and Regimes. 2nd ed. Boston: Little, Brown & Co.
Misztal, Bronislaw. 1981. "The Petite Bourgeoisie in the Socialist System." F. Bechhofer and B. Elliot, eds. The Petite Bourgeoisie: Comparative Studies of the Uneasy Stratum. London and New York: Macmillan.
Misztal, Bronislaw and Barbara A. Misztal. 1984a. "Urban Social Problems in Poland: Macro-Social Determinants." Urban Affairs Quarterly 19, No. 3.
_____. 1984b. "Unrestrained Processes in the Socialist City." Urban Affairs Quarterly [Forthcoming].
Morawski, Witold. 1983. "Samorzad pracowniczy a reform a gospodarcza." Studia Socjologiczne, (89).
Morrison, Denton E. 1971. "Some Notes Toward Theory of Relative Deprivation, Social Movements and Social Change." R. Evans, ed. Social Movements. Chicago: Rand McNally.

Nowak, Leszek. 1983. Property and Power: Towards a Non-Marxian Historical Materialism. Dodrecht and Boston: D. Reidel.
O'Connor, James. 1976. "What is Political Economy." D. Mermelstein, ed. Economics: Mainstream Readings and Radical Critiques. New York: Random House.
Pickvance, Charles G. 1983. "What is new about the new urban Sociology?" Comparative Urban Research 9 (2).
Pontusson, Jonas. 1983. "Comparative Political Economy: Sweden and France." Kapitalistate 10/11.
Poulantzas, Nicos. 1978. Political Power & Social Classes. London: Verso.
Roberts, Ron E. and Robert M. Klos. 1979. Social Movements Between the Balcony and the Barricade. St. Louis, Mo.: Mosby.
Rush, Gary B. and R. Serge Denisoff. 1971. Social and Political Movements. New York: Appleton-Century Crofts.
Smelser, Neil J. 1963. Theory of Collective Behavior. New York: Free Press.
Smith, Michael P. 1979. The City and Social Theory. New York: St. Martin's Press.
Szelenyi, Ivan. 1980. "The relative autonomy of the State or State mode of production?" A. Scott and M. Dear, eds. Urbanization and Urban Planning in Capitalist Society. New York: Methuen.
_____. 1983. Urban Inequalities Under State Socialism. Oxford and New York: Oxford University Press.
Sztompka, Piotr. 1979. Sociological Dilemmas. New York: Academic Press.
Therborn, Goran. 1980. What Does the Ruling Class Do When it Rules? London: Verso.
Touraine, Alain. 1981. The Voice and the Eye: An Analysis of Social Movements. Cambridge, Cambridge University Press.
Turner, Ralph and Lewis Killian M., eds. 1957. Collective Behavior. Englewood Cliffs, N.J.: Prentice-Hall.
Walton, John. 1979. "Urban Political Economy: A New Paradigm." Comparative Urban Research 7 (1).
Weber, Max. 1916, 1978. "Gesammelte Aufsatze Zur Soziologie und Sozial Politik." W. G. Runciman, ed., Weber. Selections in Translation. Cambridge: Cambridge University Press.
Wood, James L. and Maurice Jackson. 1982. Social Movements: Development, Participation and Dynamics. Belmont, Ca.: Wadsworth.

About the Contributors

JACK BIELASIAK is Associate Professor of Political Science at Indiana University. He specializes in analyses of contemporary Poland. His most recent work includes the volume Polish Politics: Edge of the Abyss (Praeger, 1984) that he edited jointly with Maurice Simon. In 1983-1984 Bielasiak was National Fellow at Hoover Institution for War, Revolution and Peace.

ELISABETH CRIGHTON is Associate Professor of Government at Pomona College in Claremont, California. Her work centers around contemporary political movements with special focus on Northern Ireland.

PAUL G. LEWIS is Senior Lecturer in Government at the Open University in England. He is an expert on the Communist Party (PUWP) in Poland and on power relations in socialist society. His most recent publications include "Institutionalization and political change in Poland" (in The State and Socialist Society, edited by N. Harding, Albany: SUNY Press, 1984) and "Legitimacy and the Polish Communist State" (in States and Societies, edited by D. Held et al., Oxford: Martin Robertson, 1983).

ROBERT MANCHIN is visiting Research Fellow at the University of Wisconsin and Research Associate at the Institute of Sociology, Hungarian Academy of Sciences in Budapest. He specializes in political and economic sociology.

MARIA MARKUS, born in Poland, educated at the Lomonosov University in Moscow, was research fellow at the Institute of Philosophy, Hungarian Academy of Sciences. A member of the "Budapest School" of Marxism and founding member of the Institute of Sociology, she eventually lost her academic position in 1977. She specializes in the sociology of work, political sociology, and stratification. Widely published in international journals, she has coauthored several scholarly books, including Political Legitimation in Communist States (St. Martin's Press, 1982) and contributed to Telos, Thesis Eleven, and Australian and New Zealand Journal of Sociology. She is currently Senior Lecturer in Sociology at the University of New South Wales in Australia.

BARBARA A. MISZTAL, born and educated in Poland, was Assistant Professor at the Institute of Philosophy and Sociology, Academy of Sciences in Warsaw. She specializes in urban and political sociology, and has widely published in leading professional journals in Poland. Her recent publications are "Urban Social Problems in Poland. Macro-Social Determinants" (Urban Affairs Quarterly, 1984), and "Transformation of Polish Political Elites" (Contemporary Polish Politics: At The Edge of the Abyss, Praeger, 1984) co-authored with Bronislaw Misztal. She is currently Visiting Lecturer in Sociology at the University of California, Riverside.

BRONISLAW MISZTAL, born and educated in Poland, was Associate Professor of Sociology at the Institute of Philosophy and Sociology, Academy of Sciences in Warsaw. He specializes in social movements theory, political participation, and urban political sociology. His major publications are: Peer-Groups in Urban Social Structure (in Polish, Ossolineum, 1974), Problems of Social Participation and Cooperation (in Polish, Ossolineum, 1977), Urban Sociology (in Polish, IWCRZZ, 1978) and Poland: A Sociological Portrait (forthcoming from Frances Pinter in 1985). He has contributed to Urban Affairs Quarterly, International Journal of Oral History, and several collective volumes. Former holder of the Jacques Leclercq Chair at Catholic University of Louvain, and Senior Fulbright Scholar at the University of Chicago, he taught at Washington University (St. Louis), Southern Illinois University, Carbondale and is currently Visiting Professor at Pitzer College, The Claremont Colleges.

IVAN SZELENYI, born and educated in Hungary, was Research Associate at the Institute of Sociology, Hungarian Academy of Sciences where he specialized in urban studies. His major publications are: Intellectuals on the Road to Class Power, co-authored with George Konrad (Harcourt and Brace, 1979) and Urban Inequalities Under State Socialism (Oxford University Press, 1983). He also edited Urban Policies of the New Right: Critical Responses (Sage, 1984) and contributed to the American Sociological Review, American Journal of Sociology, Theory and Society, International Journal of Urban and Regional Research, and other scholarly journals. Former Foundation Professor of Sociology at Flinders University in South Australia, he is currently Professor of Sociology at the University of Wisconsin.

BOGDAN SZAJKOWSKI, born and educated in Poland, conducted his postgraduate studies at Kings College, Cambridge. His writing on contemporary Communist affairs has appeared in professional journals worldwide. Among his major publications are: Marxist

Governments. A World Survey (Macmillan, 1981), The Establishments of Marxist Regimes (Butterworths, 1982) and Next to God . . . Poland (Frances Pinter, 1983). He is the editor of Communist Affairs and a consultant to Independent Television News network in Britain. He has taught at the Australian National University in Canberra, University College in Dublin, Calgary University in Canada, and is currently Lecturer in Comparative Social Institutions at University College in Cardiff.

SCOTT WARREN teaches at Pomona College in Claremont, California. His work in political theory, art theory, and philosophy grows out of an interest in phenomenology, existentialism, critical theory, and neo-Marxism. His book, The Emergence of Dialectical Theory: Philosophy and Political Inquiry, has recently been published by the University of Chicago Press (1984).

083065
20/10/87
CLIO PRESS LTD